GREAT MOMENTS OF BASEBALL

In the great game of baseball, certain electric moments boil up unpredictably, bring the fans screaming to their feet and become an unforgettable part of the sport's colorful history. Beginning with that classic 1920 World Series clincher between the Cleveland Indians and the Brooklyn Dodgers, when Bill Wambsganss pulled off the rarest play in baseball, sportswriter Larry Bortstein highlights the truly great moments of over fifty years—games when a cellar team had been given up for dead only to win over unbelievable odds, games when a star suddenly became a superstar right before the eyes of sixty thousand fans.

Here is a book that recreates those thrilling moments so graphically that you will share all their excitement and tension—from the crack of the Babe's bat when he called his shot at Wrigley Field, down the years to Roberto Clemente's three thousandth, and last, hit.

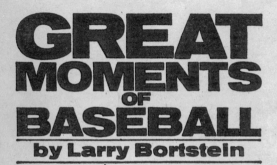

GREAT MOMENTS OF BASEBALL
by Larry Bortstein

tempo books

GROSSET & DUNLAP

Publishers   New York

ISBN: 0-448-05568-6
Tempo Books is registered in the U. S. Patent Office
Published simultaneously in Canada

A Tempo Books Original

Printed in the United States of America

TO STEVEN

My little slugger

ACKNOWLEDGMENT

The author is grateful for research assistance supplied by Morris Alpern and Robert Elkin, and also wishes to thank Seymour Siwoff, director of the Elias Sports Bureau. Particularly worthy of praise are the players who have provided baseball with countless great moments for more than 100 years, and the authors who have chronicled them.

CONTENTS

1920 World Series

No World Series ever began under a darker cloud than the 1920 classic between the Cleveland Indians and Brooklyn Dodgers, and no American League champion ever carried its league's banner into a World Series with more pressure riding on the outcome than did those 1920 Indians.

The Tribe, managed by Tris Speaker, who also was the team's star player, had one of the finest all-round clubs in the history of the junior circuit. However, it is very likely that they would never have won their first pennant were it not for the late-season disclosure that the White Sox had conspired to lose the 1919 World Series to Cincinnati. Eight Chicago players were suspended by Commissioner Kenesaw Mountain Landis, though the Sox were in the midst of a heated struggle for the pennant with the New York Yankees and the Indians.

Cleveland capitalized on the loss of eight of Chicago's key performers, and finally sneaked home in first place, two games ahead of the White Sox, and another length ahead of the Yankees, who were just beginning to build their American League dynasty.

Weeks before they finally clinched the pennant, the Indians had been victimized by one of the most tragic episodes in baseball history. On August 16, their star shortstop, Ray Chapman, had been struck in the head by a pitch from Carl Mays of the Yankees. Mays threw his pitches with an underhand motion and Chapman virtually stepped into one of his deliveries. Chapman was removed unconscious from the field and taken to a New York hospital. He died the next morning without ever regaining consciousness, the first and only major leaguer to meet death on the playing field.

Chapman, a fine, popular performer, was sorely missed by the Indians in the final crucial weeks of the pennant chase. He had been batting .303 at the time of his fatal beaning, which was recorded officially as an accident. Mays, the pitcher, was exonerated of all blame. Cleveland managed to obtain a young shortstop named Joe Sewell for the final few games, and Sewell went on to a great major league career. Ironically, the man who was the regular second baseman for the Indians in 1920, Bill Wambsganss, came to Cleveland as a shortstop, but had been switched to second base because Chapman was a fixture at short.

Speaker, the manager, was adept at platooning his players, and finally shuffled and shuttled the Indians home in front, with no small thanks to Speaker himself, a great centerfielder. Tris led the Cleveland batters with a remarkable .388 average, and five other Indian regulars batted over .300, as did a couple of second-stringers. Overall, the club finished the regular season with a .303 average.

The Indians had excellent pitching, too. There was Jim Bagby, a right-hander who won 31 games. Two other right-handers, Stan Coveleskie and Ray Caldwell, won twenty-four and twenty games, respectively. Southpaw Walter (Duster) Mails, who could throw a blazing fastball, joined the club late in the year and recorded seven victories without a single defeat. Handling this corps of outstanding pitchers was Steve O'Neill, later a highly successful major league manager and rated an expert at handling pitchers.

Despite their many obvious credentials, the Indians were considered a question mark by experts as they

entered the World Series against the National League
champion Dodgers.

The Brooklyn club, usually downtrodden in past
years, had captured the National League flag by seven
games over the runner-up New York Giants. Wilbert
"Uncle Robbie" Robinson managed the club that had
seven top returning players from the 1916 National
League titlists, the only other time the Dodgers had
won the pennant. These stars included outfielder Zack
Wheat, catcher Otto Miller, shortstop Ivy Olson, and
pitchers Rube Marquard and Sherry Smith. Brooklyn
newcomers included right-handed spitball specialist
Burleigh Grimes, a twenty-three-game winner during the
regular season; first baseman Ed Konetchy and second
baseman Pete Kilduff.

These Dodgers figured to give Tris Speaker's Indians
a tough struggle in the World Series, which then was
contested as a best-five-of-nine-games tournament. The
first three games were scheduled to be played in Brooklyn, and the Dodgers hoped to get off to a good start
before their home fans.

Baseball still was reeling from the stench of the
late-season disclosures about the White Sox' having
"thrown" the 1919 Series. But interest in the 1920 pro-
ceedings ran high in the two contesting cities, and neither team had difficulty filling its relatively small ballpark, Ebbets Field in Brooklyn and old League Park
in Cleveland. The Series opened before 23,573 fans on
a chilly Tuesday afternoon, October 5.

Brooklyn's hopes for getting off to a fast start were
dashed when Coveleskie outpitched Marquard in a duel
of five-hitters, 3-1. But the Dodgers got even the following afternoon when Grimes, making his Series debut,
shut out the Tribe with only seven hits, 3-0. Bagby
was the losing pitcher for Cleveland.

Brooklyn took a two-to-one Series lead the next day

behind Sherry Smith, who yielded but three hits in fashioning a 2-1 triumph. Smith, a left-hander, got all the runs he needed when the Dodgers drove Cleveland's Caldwell from the mound with a two-run first inning.

After a day off for travel, the teams resumed hostilities on Saturday, October 9, in Cleveland. Right-hander Jeff Pfeffer was sent to the mound by Dodger manager Robinson to try to pitch Brooklyn into a 3-1 Series lead. But Pfeffer was no match for Coveleskie, who spun his second victory of the Series, 5-1.

Thus the stage was set for one of the most bizarre games in baseball history. It used to be said for many years in Brooklyn that "everything happens to the Dodgers." The expression might have had its origin on Sunday, October 10, 1920, in Cleveland, when not only could everything happen to the Dodgers: everything did.

The opposing pitchers were Bagby for the Indians and Grimes for the Dodgers. The Cleveland hurler retired the Brooklyns routinely in the top of the first. Events in the Indian half of the inning were anything but routine.

Charlie Jamieson, Cleveland's leftfielder, led off with a scratch hit to the infield. Wambsganss followed with a single, moving Jamieson to second. Speaker went up to sacrifice, but beat out the resulting bunt to fill the bases.

This brought up Elmer Smith, the left-handed-batting rightfielder of the Indians. A .316 hitter during the season, Smith represented the major power threat for Cleveland in this pre-lively ball era. The 28-year-old native of Sandusky, Ohio, clouted 12 homers in 1920, tops among the Indians.

Grimes worked carefully on Smith and slipped over two strikes. But Elmer then got hold of a spitball and lofted it high over the rightfield wall, as the Cleveland fans let loose a roar that carried far out on Lake Erie.

Grimes finally retired the side, but the damage had been done—four Indian runs, on the strength of Smith's grand slam home run, the first in World Series history.

As if that weren't enough, pitcher Bagby was in such a merry mood by his turn at bat in the fourth inning that he promptly belted out a three-run homer off another Grimes spitball. Indian first baseman Doc Johnston and catcher Steve O'Neill were on base when Bagby unloaded the first homer ever hit by a pitcher in a Series game. That blow made it 7-0 in favor of Cleveland and finished Grimes for the day.

Further indignities awaited the Dodgers in their half of the fifth. The Indians took the field with a big lead, the first time either team had opened up a commanding margin at any time in the Series. The Cleveland defense lined up with Jamieson, Speaker and Smith in the outfield, Johnston at first, Larry Gardner at third, Joe Sewell at short, O'Neill behind the plate, Bagby on the mound—and Bill Wambsganss at second base.

Better known as "Wamby," Bill was born in Cleveland in 1894, but moved with his family to Fort Wayne, Indiana, when he was a small child. The senior Wambsganss was a Lutheran clergyman of Dutch descent, who hoped that his son would someday also enter the ministry.

When he was old enough, Bill entered Concordia College in Fort Wayne to prepare for the religious calling. But baseball soon became his dominant activity.

"Once I got to playing on the college team," Wambsganss recalled many years later, "all I did was sit in the classroom and look out the window, wishing that class was over so I could go out and play ball.

"I didn't see how I could possibly become a minister," Wamby went on. "I just wasn't any good at speaking in front of people. I simply couldn't do it."

Bill was the recipient of good fortune in 1913. By this time, he had convinced his father that he really didn't want to become a minister, and that he preferred baseball. One of the other students at Concordia College had played some minor league ball and one day received a letter from a friend who was managing a team in Cedar Rapids, Iowa. The friend was asking the student if he could recommend a shortstop. The seminarian recommended Wamby, and Bill was on his way in professional baseball, beginning with the Cedar Rapids club of the Central Association. The next year, 1914, Wamby came up with the Indians.

Going into the 1920 World Series, Wambsganss hadn't done much to distinguish himself that season. He had the lowest batting average of all Cleveland regulars, .244, a drop of thirty-four points from his 1919 average of .278. Despite his weak bat, Bill played in 153 of the Indians' 154 games. His work at second base was outstanding.

Blessed with his 7-0 lead, Cleveland pitcher Bagby seemed to relax a bit as he faced the Dodger batters in the top of the fifth inning of the fifth game in the 1920 Series. The first two men to face him, Kilduff and Miller, reached base safely.

This brought up Clarence Mitchell, who had relieved Grimes on the mound for Brooklyn after Bagby's homer in the third inning. Mitchell, like Grimes, was a spitball pitcher, with this difference; Mitchell was the only *left-handed* spitball pitcher in the majors at that time.

He also was a good hitter, so Dodger manager Robinson let him bat for himself though Brooklyn was trailing badly. Robinson signaled for the hit-and-run, meaning that both baserunners would be running with the pitch from Bagby to Mitchell.

The Cleveland infield was playing deep and shaded to the right side for Mitchell, a left-handed pull hit-

ter. With nobody out, the Indians might have been expected to be setting themselves for a double play pos-
sibility. But with a seven-run lead, they probably could
afford to act a little cavalier about the situation.

Mitchell slashed at a Bagby pitch and sent it on a
rising line toward centerfield, a little to the right of
Wambsganss, who was playing between first and second. Wamby leaped high for the ball and barely
managed to reach high enough to snare it in his gloved
hand.

The impetus of Wambsganss' run and leap had carried him over toward second base, where Pete Kilduff
had just recently been stationed. The Dodger second
baseman, believing that Mitchell's blow was a certain
base hit, now was heading towards third. All Wamby
had to do to retire Kilduff was to step on second base.
He did just that.

Meanwhile, Otto Miller, sensing that something was
terribly wrong, stood with his mouth hanging open,
midway between first and second. Wambsganss had
only to move to his left a few steps to tag Miller on
the right shoulder. As soon as he did, the Indian second baseman started running into the dugout.

Wamby was one of the few men in the stadium who
realized what had just taken place. It all happened so
suddenly that most of the fans and almost all the players were at a loss to explain what had happened.

It was, of course, a triple play, an *unassisted* triple
play, the rarest play in baseball. In all of baseball history through 1972, only eight unassisted triple plays
have been recorded in the major leagues, including Bill
Wambsganss' gem. Wamby's still stands as the only unassisted triple play ever pulled in a World Series game.

The Dodgers certainly must have taken the hint
that 1920 wasn't going to be their year to win the World
Series. They finally reached Bagby for a run in the

ninth inning, but it was far too little and too late to prevent an 8-1 defeat. That ninth-inning run was the last the Dodgers scored in the Series. They submitted meekly in the next two games, losing both by shutouts. "Duster" Mails stopped them, 1-0 in the sixth game, and then Coveleskie won his third game of the classic, a five-hit 3-0 blanking. Cleveland was the champion of the baseball world, five games to two.

Wambsganss lasted in the major leagues until 1926. In later years he complained that, despite his 13 years in the big time, the only thing anybody ever remembered about him was his unassisted triple play against Brooklyn in the 1920 World Series.

There have been many hundreds of players who enjoyed better overall careers in the majors than Wambsganss, yet have been totally forgotten with the passing of time. Wamby's play never will be forgotten, nor will the other Wamby incidents in the fifth game of the 1920 World Series.

Sunday, October 10, 1920, at Cleveland

Brooklyn (N)	AB.	R.	H.	Cleveland (A)	AB.	R.	H.
Olson, ss	4	0	2	Jamieson, lf	4	1	2
Sheehan, 3b	3	0	1	*Graney, lf	1	0	0
Griffith, rf	4	0	0	Wambsganss, 2b	5	1	1
Wheat, lf	4	1	2	Speaker, cf	3	2	1
Myers, cf	4	0	2	E. Smith, rf	4	1	3
Konetchy, 1b	4	0	2	Gardner, 3b	4	0	1
Kilduff, 2b	4	0	1	W. Johnston, 1b	3	1	2
Miller, c	2	0	0	Sewell, ss	3	0	0
Krueger, c	2	0	1	O'Neill, c	2	1	0
Grimes, p	1	0	0	Thomas, c	0	0	0
Mitchell, p	2	0	0	Bagby, p	4	1	2
Totals	34	1	13	Totals	33	8	12

Brooklyn .... 0 0 0 0 0 0 0 0 1—1
Cleveland .... 4 0 0 3 1 0 0 0 *—8

*Struck out for Jamieson in eighth. Runs batted in—E. Smith 4, Bagby 3, Gardner, Konetchy. Three-base hits—Konetchy, E. Smith. Home Runs—E. Smith, Bagby. Sacrifice hits—Sheehan, W. Johnston. Double plays—Olson, Kilduff and Konetchy; Jamieson and O'Neill; Gardner, Wambsganss and W. Johnston; W. Johnston, Sewell and W. Johnston. Triple play—Wambsganss, unassisted. Left on bases—Brooklyn 7, Cleveland 6. Earned runs—Cleveland 7, Brooklyn 1. Struck out—By Bagby 3, by Mitchell 1. Bases on balls—Off Grimes 1, off Mitchell 3. Wild pitch—Bagby. Hits—Off Grimes 9 in 3 1/3 innings, off Mitchell 3 in 4 2/3 innings. Passed ball—Miller. Losing pitcher—Grimes. Umpires—Klem (N. L.), Connolly (A. L.), O'Day (N. L.) and Dinneen (A. L.). Time—1:49. Attendance—26,884.

The Babe Calls His Shot

The reign of George Herman "Babe" Ruth as baseball's "Sultan of Swat" was beginning to topple in 1932. At the age of 37 the fabulous Babe had left his best years behind him. The round-faced man with the round belly and matchstick legs had hammered his historic 60 home runs in 1927, and in 1928 he had achieved a record .625 batting average in the World Series against the St. Louis Cardinals and had belted three homers in one Series game.

During the peak years of his 22-year major league career Ruth had compiled records that bordered on the unbelievable. His feats of longball hitting made him the supreme star of baseball, and the hero of youth throughout America. Babe grew up as an orphan at St. Mary's Industrial School in his hometown of Baltimore, where he was taught to be a tailor. As the greatest baseball star of his time, he was worshipped by youngsters, particularly those who grew up in the same unfortunate circumstances that marred his own boyhood.

Even as his talents began to wane, Babe still was the Babe, playing the game to the hilt. In 1932, he still managed a prodigious .341 batting average and 41 home runs, although for the first time in seven seasons, he lost the American League homer title. That honor fell to Jimmie Foxx of the Philadelphia Athletics, who approached, but couldn't match, Ruth's one-season record of 60 circuit blasts. Foxx had to be content with 58.

Despite his decline, Babe still was the most feared batter in baseball as his New York Yankees faced the Chicago Cubs in the 1932 World Series.

The Yankees, who had recaptured the American League pennant from Philadelphia after a three-year hold by the A's, were heavily favored to defeat the Cubs in the postseason competition. And the New Yorkers demonstrated their strength by winning the first two games at New York, 12-6 and 5-2. Ruth had a single in each game and drove in two Yankee runs in the opener.

When the scene shifted to Chicago for the third game, the Cubs did much better. Before 49,986 Windy City fans gathered in Wrigley Field, the Cubs rallied from a 4-1 deficit to tie the score in the fourth inning. In the first inning Ruth accounted for three quick New York runs when he connected for a home run with two men on base. It was a long drive into the centerfield bleachers and the Bronx Bombers appeared on the verge of another runaway victory. But the Cubs had fought back courageously.

When the Babe came up to bat in the top of the fifth inning, there were no Yankee runners on base. The Cub fans, frustrated by their team's defeats in the first two games but now given a reason to cheer, booed Ruth lustily. The boos rose as the familiar figure with the big number 3 on the back of his uniform stepped into the left-handed batter's box. They continued even as the Babe took a few practice swings with his 42-ounce bat, one of the heaviest weapons ever swung in major league baseball.

Babe stood at the plate without hearing the taunts. He looked straight ahead at the pitcher, right-hander Charlie Root, a 15-game winner for Chicago during the regular season. Root had been the victim of Ruth's first-inning home run, but had retired him in his second plate appearance.

By this time the Cub players had joined the fans in tossing barbs at the Babe. In the age-old tradition of bench-jockeying, the Cubs hinted that perhaps Babe was getting too old for this young man's game.

Bench-jockeying had been a feature of the 1932 World Series from its inception at Yankee Stadium. Mark Koenig, a one-time Yankee shortstop, had been sold to the Cubs during the season and had played a major role in the pennant drive by the Chicagoans. They prevailed over the Pittsburgh Pirates by four games at the conclusion of the 154-game schedule. But Koenig's Chicago teammates voted Koenig only half a share of World Series money.

The first time Ruth ran into Koenig at the Stadium, he greeted his former teammate warmly. Then he added, loud enough for the other Cubs to hear, "Some cheapskates you play with, Mark!"

From that moment, the Cubs heckled Ruth with vigor. Their apparent intention was to upset him.

But the Babe didn't upset easily. In the batter's box he looked into the Cub dugout, eyeing his tormentors, then spun around to catcher Gabby Hartnett, who was in his crouch ready to receive Root's delivery.

"If he throws one in here," Ruth said to Hartnett, "I'll hit it out again."

Finally Root threw a pitch. It was a good pitch, across the heart of the plate. But the Babe let it go by for a called strike. More boos erupted from the packed stands. Ruth held up one finger indicating that the pitch had, indeed, been one strike.

As Root threw his second pitch Babe remained motionless at the plate. Again the pitch flew across the plate for a called strike. Ruth held up his finger again to indicate another strike as boos poured from the stands and the Cub players continued their taunts.

Then the Babe pointed in the direction of the mound, where Root was chuckling to himself. Ruth had a habit of calling everyone "keed" or "kid." He yelled out at Root, "You still need one more, keed!"

This said, Ruth extended his right arm toward the centerfield fence. That gesture has become one of the most controversial incidents in baseball history. What was the Babe's actual intent in pointing toward the fence? Was he advising the world that he would blast the next pitch from Root over that .fence? Was he simply reminding Root that the pitcher still needed to get one more strike before Ruth would have to walk back to the dugout, a strikeout victim?

Probably no one will ever really know. Did Babe call his shot? Perhaps. What is certain, however, is that Ruth unleashed his powerful swing at Root's next offering and sent the ball exploding like a rocket high into the Chicago sky. It didn't come to rest until it had sailed past the flagpole in centerfield, 436 feet from home plate—in the very area toward which Ruth had seemed to point before the pitch.

Root, recreating the incident many years later, recalled that he had considered "wasting" his third pitch to Ruth, intentionally throwing a bad pitch in the hope that an overanxious Babe would be swinging wildly.

"I figured Ruth would be thinking that way too," said Root. "So I decided to cross him up and come in with my best pitch."

As the Babe circled the bases after his blast, he made it a point to address every Cub infielder. He taunted Chicago's playing manager Charlie Grimm, who was stationed at first base. Then he teased Billy Herman at second base, laughed wickedly at shortstop Billy Jurges and shot a final kidding chide at third baseman Woody English.

The crowd, intensely partisan on behalf of the Cubs scant seconds earlier, couldn't fail to appreciate the historic incident it had just witnessed. The boos had changed to loud cheers for the Babe.

The Yankees scored another run in the top of the fifth, driving Root from the game and taking a 6-4 lead. New York finally won the game, 7-5, and in the Cub locker room after the contest, Root, the victimized pitcher, sat slumped on a stool in front of his locker.

"That man isn't human," Root mumbled, echoing a statement many others before him had made about the incredible Babe.

Back at the Yankees' hotel, Ruth was greeted by a mob of reporters. "Suppose you had missed hitting a homer?" one reporter asked the Babe. "You would have looked like the biggest chump of all time, wouldn't you?"

"I guess so," shrugged the Babe. "But I never even thought about it. I guess nobody but a fool would have done what I did, but I got mad and I just wanted to hit that ball hard . . . somewhere."

The next day the Yankees completed a four-game sweep of the World Series, routing the Cubs, 13-6. Ruth's only contribution to a 19-hit New York attack was a single that drove in a run. The more than 49,000 fans who filled Wrigley Field for this game couldn't have known it at the time, but they were watching the Babe's final World Series appearance.

Ruth played two more seasons with the Yankees, continuing his inevitable slide downhill, and the Yankees failed to win the pennant either time. By 1935, the Babe was playing out the string as a part-time performer for the Boston Braves. As a Brave, he belted the last six of his record total of 714 home runs, including three in a single game against the Pirates on

May 25, 1935. That was the Babe's farewell to baseball, and what a farewell it was!

Ruth appeared in four more games after that final barrage of three homers but failed to hit safely. On June 2, 1935, the Babe announced his retirement.

He didn't fulfill an ambition he had treasured—to play in one more World Series. But he had made his last postseason appearance a memorable one.

That home run Babe called—or didn't call—in the third game of the 1932 World Series was his fifteenth —and last—in World Series competition.

Saturday, October 1, 1932, at Chicago

New York (A)	AB.	R.	H.	Chicago (N)	AB.	R.	H.
Combs, cf	5	1	0	Herman, 2b	4	1	0
Sewell, 3b	2	1	0	English, 3b	4	0	0
RUTH, lf	4	2	2	Cuyler, rf	4	1	3
Gehrig, 1b	5	2	2	Stephenson, lf	4	0	1
Lazzeri, 2b	4	1	0	Moore, cf	3	1	0
Dickey, c	4	0	1	Grimm, 1b	4	0	1
Chapman, rf	4	0	2	Hartnett, c	4	1	1
Crosetti, ss	4	0	1	Jurges, ss	4	1	3
Pipgras, p	5	0	0	Root, p	2	0	0
Pennock, p	0	0	0	Malone, p	0	0	0
				aGudat	1	0	0
Totals	37	7	8	May, p	0	0	0
				Tinning, p	0	0	0
				bKoenig	0	0	0
				cHemsley	1	0	0
				Totals	35	5	9

aPopped out for Malone in seventh
bAnnounced for Tinning in ninth
cStruck out for Koenig in ninth

New York .... 3 0 1   0 2 0   0 0 1—7
Chicago .... 1 0 2   1 0 0   0 0 1—5

Runs batted in—Ruth 4, Gehrig 2, Cuyler 2, Grimm, Chapman, Hartnett. Two-base hits—Chapman, Cuyler, Jurges, Grimm. Home runs—Ruth 2, Gehrig 2, Cuyler, Hartnett. Stolen base—Jurges. Double plays—Sewell, Lazzeri and Gehrig; Herman, Jurges and Grimm. Left on bases—New York 11, Chicago 6. Earned runs—New York 5, Chicago 4. Strikeouts—Root 4, Malone 4, May 1, Tinning 1, Pipgras 1, Pennock 1. Bases on balls—Root 3, Malone 4, Pipgras 3. Hit by pitcher—by May (Sewell). Hits off—Root 6 in 4 1/3 innings; Malone 1 in 2 2/3; May 1 in 1 1/3; Tinning 0 in 2/3; Pipgras 9 in 8 (pitched to two batters in ninth); Pennock 0 in 1. Winning pitcher—Pipgras. Losing pitcher—Root. Umpires—Van Graflan, Magerkurth, Dinneen, Klem. Time—2:11. Attendance—49,986.

Joe DiMaggio Hits In 56 Straight Games

What has been the most heroic feat in the history of baseball? The most extraordinary accomplishment? When professional baseball marked its one-hundredth anniversary in 1969, *Sport* Magazine attempted to find an answer to these questions. The magazine's editors signed the late Lee Allen, historian of the National Baseball Hall of Fame and Museum in Cooperstown, New York, to conduct a survey of leading baseball authorities.

Allen contacted more than 300 people in baseball —members of the Hall of Fame, other star players, club owners, general managers, field managers, coaches, umpires and scouts—men who had devoted their lives to the game. To each of these men, Allen put the question: what have been the top three individual accomplishments in baseball history, listed in order of preference?

The result? An overwhelming victory for Joe Di-Maggio who, from May 15 through July 16, 1941, hit safely in fifty-six consecutive games for the New York Yankees. DiMaggio received more than twice the number of votes for his achievement than runner-up Babe Ruth received for his feat of sixty home runs in 1927.

This verdict surprised almost no one. Most fans of baseball had suspected for years that the DiMaggio feat was without precedent in baseball history, indeed in all of sports history. Most great athletic accomplishments involve the setting of a record at one particular moment in time, such as winning a track event in the fastest clocking ever posted, or over an extended, indefinite amount of time, such as Babe Ruth's sixty homers, spread across the entire 1927 season. But DiMaggio's 56-game consecutive hitting streak had the ultimate element of difficulty: in order to maintain his mark, Joe, the great Yankee centerfielder, had to get a hit, some kind of hit, every single day, for more than two months. A man seeking a one-season record for home runs can go one, two, or more days without hitting a ball out of the park. He can catch up by hitting two homers in one game. But DiMaggio's mark is without parallel in sports history.

They called him "The Yankee Clipper" when he played in New York. Though he was shy and lacked the polish and poise he developed in his later years, Joe D., as he also was known, was the acknowledged leader of the Yankees, the most powerful team in baseball during most of DiMaggio's thirteen seasons with the club.

There almost was no career in major league baseball for Joe, though he grew up as the best of three ballplaying brothers from the Fisherman's Wharf section of San Francisco. Two of Joe's brothers, Dominic and Vincent, also reached the majors, an astonishing feat for one family, the family of Giuseppe and Rosalie DiMaggio.

In the nineteen-thirties, Giuseppe DiMaggio had a fishing boat with which he eked out a living for his family of nine children. There were five boys altogether, and four girls. Giuseppe DiMaggio's father before him had made his living as a fisherman in Sicily, as had his father and his father before that. For several generations, the DiMaggios of Sicily had lived off the sea. When Giuseppe DiMaggio came to the United States, he joined many other Italian immigrants who had settled around Fisherman's Wharf.

Joseph Paul DiMaggio was born November 25, 1914, and from the earliest days of his boyhood, he could not imagine himself following in the seafaring tradition of his family. In fact, the sight and smell of the sea and the fish repelled Joe as a boy. Nothing else interested Joe much as a youngster either, not even baseball, though he was adept at the game, more adept than his older brother Vince, who already had major league aspirations. Vince was playing for the minor league team in San Francisco and waiting for what he hoped would be the purchase of his contract by a major league club. There was no major league ball on the west coast at that time. There was no team in the majors farther west than St. Louis.

Vince finally convinced Joe, two years younger than himself, to try out for the San Francisco club. Reluctantly, Joe tried out and was so sensational that he took away the centerfielding job that had belonged to Vince, who was sold to another team. Joe quickly became the outstanding player in the minor leagues and the future seemed unlimited for the young man in his early twenties. Major league scouts clamored for his signature on a contract.

One day Joe stepped out of an automobile and something happened to his knee. "It popped like a pistol," he recalled in later years. "The pain was so bad I could hardly stand up. I went to a doctor that night and he told me I had pulled a lot of tendons. The knee didn't feel right for a long time after that."

In truth, Joe's knee never was completely "right" again. Even after he had reached the major leagues and become a star of the first rank, Joe had difficulty with the knee and saw that it received constant and proper attention.

After he first tore up his knee, Joe discovered that a lot of major league scouts had lost interest in him.

Knees can be unpredictable, and many scouts were now uncertain of Joe's future as a ballplayer.

The Yankees didn't lose interest in DiMaggio. They bought his contract from San Francisco and ordered him to report to training camp in Florida in the spring of 1936.

Rarely has the advent of a rookie ever been more anxiously awaited than was DiMaggio's. The Yankees had slipped from their customary perch on top of the American League standings. For three straight years they had failed to win the pennant, a major slump by their lofty standards. Babe Ruth was gone, and though Lou Gehrig still was a star, the Yankees needed an infusion of new blood.

DiMaggio was the new blood. He was an immediate sensation. As a rookie he made the American League All-Star team. He batted .323 and belted 29 home runs. He played centerfield in mammoth Yankee Stadium as if the position had been invented for him. The Bronx Bombers raced to the American League championship and a victory in six games over the Giants in the 1936 World Series. Joe batted .346 in the fall classic. Yankee Stadium denizens had a new idol in this lean, long-legged, heavy-thighed, long-nosed silent young man.

The Yankees won pennants and World Series in 1937, 1938 and 1939, as DiMaggio emerged as the dominant player in baseball. He led the league with 46 homers in '37, hammered thirty-two circuits in '38 and topped American League batsmen in average in '39 with a .381 mark.

In 1940 the Yankees fell to third place. Gehrig was now gone, fatally ill, and Joe was unable to carry the offensive burden by himself, though he did manage his second consecutive batting title with a .352 average. It seemed, however, that the Yankees were fading as a team.

They began slowly again in 1941. DiMaggio was twenty-six years old, 6-2, 200 pounds, supposedly at the peak of his career. The press was calling him "The Great Man." But in the early weeks of the 1941 campaign even "The Great Man" was in a slump. When Mel Harder of the Cleveland Indians set Joe down without a hit in three official times at bat on May 14, Joe's average for his last thirteen games dwindled to .237, 108 points below his five-year major League norm of .345.

"I'm lunging and hitting some on the handle," he explained, "and when I start pressing it gets worse. There's no cure. It just takes time to come out of it."

The next day, May 15, DiMaggio came out of it a little with a first-inning single off Chicago southpaw Edgar Smith. But Joe was retired in his three other times at bat, and the White Sox trounced the New Yorkers, 13-1. The Yankees were limping along in fourth place, struggling to keep their record at the .500 level. It was one of the slowest starts in history for the once invincible Bombers.

And that's the way DiMaggio's streak built up too—slowly, without fanfare. In its early days hardly anyone paid attention to it. Though nobody could have guessed it at the time, Joe's three hitless trips against the Indians' Harder on May 14 represented his last game without a hit for a period of two months and three days.

It wasn't until he had hit safely in eighteen straight games that the New York *Times* thought to mention the fact. But when DiMaggio passed thirty games in a row, when he started to close in on the records—George Sisler's modern mark of forty-one straight games and Wee Willie Keeler's 1897 record of forty-four straight games—people began to take notice. Suddenly, the whole country, even people with no interest whatever in baseball, began watching and keeping track of Joe's streak.

Press boxes in every city where baseball was played kept track as DiMaggio kept hitting. Newspapers ran a front-page box every day telling readers how Joe had done the previous day. This service wasn't fast enough for many fans. Switchboards lit up in newspaper offices every afternoon that the Yankees were playing, with callers asking the question: "Did DiMaggio get his hit yet?" Radio broadcasts were interrupted constantly by bulletins charting Joe's progress. Players all over the major leagues got into the habit of looking up into the press boxes for bulletin signals. One congressman in Washington, D. C. hired a pageboy whose sole function it was to rush the latest information on DiMaggio's streak to the floor of the House.

Things really began getting interesting after Joe had passed Rogers Hornsby's National League record of thirty-three straight games. DiMaggio now was the target of every pitcher and every team in the American League, each striving to be the one to finally halt the long streak.

By June 28, the streak had reached thirty-nine games and DiMaggio and the Yankees were facing the Philadelphia Athletics. The A's had a pitcher named Johnny Babich, who had vowed to stop Joe.

"Babich had tried out with us the year before," DiMaggio recalled, "but the club sent him down. Then he caught on with the A's and he beat us five times. Well, he was still sore, and he seemed to think that if he stopped me, even if he walked me four times, he would be rubbing it in. My first time up against Babich, his first three pitches were high and wide. I got the hit sign but I couldn't have reached the fourth pitch with a ten-foot pole. The second time up, it was the same thing. Ball one, ball two, ball three. But then he gave me one I could get to, and I knocked him on the seat of his pants. It went for a double."

The very next day in Washington, the streak nearly came to an end at forty. It was an unbearably hot afternoon in the nation's capital and the Yankees were meeting the Senators in a doubleheader. If DiMaggio could get a hit in each game, he would pass Sisler's mark of forty-one straight games.

Dutch Leonard, a knuckleballer, pitched the opening game for the Senators, and his fluttery deliveries retired Joe in his first two at-bats. In the top of the sixth, DiMaggio faced Leonard for the third time.

Joe liked the first pitch and swung at it—but missed. The next one went by for a ball. The third pitch was a fastball and Joe timed it well and sent it rocketing out on a line to left-centerfield. Doc Cramer, the Washington leftfielder, and George Case, the centerfielder, gave chase to the ball, which seemed destined to go well past them.

But Case, a very fast man who always ranked among the leading base-stealers in the American League, nearly caught up with the ball. He leaped, but it bounced off his glove as he hit the ground, and rolled all the way to the wall for a DiMaggio double. Had Case succeeded in making a miraculous catch, Joe's streak would have been over, as he went out easily in his last plate appearance of the game.

But that double off Leonard had enabled DiMaggio to tie Sisler's record. In the second game of the doubleheader Joe got a single off a big right-hander named Arnold "Red" Anderson to surpass Sisler's mark.

Next DiMaggio went after Keeler's forty-four-year-old record of forty-four consecutive games. Joe tied Keeler with three hits in a doubleheader against the Boston Red Sox on July 1. Then, on July 2, against a 31-year-old Boston rookie right-hander named Heber

"Dick" Newsome, DiMaggio homered to go past the Keeler standard.

Now Joe felt release from the tension and he began to hit even better. He would close out his streak by collecting twenty-six hits in forty-three trips to the plate, an astounding .605 pace. On July 11, he reached the fifty mark, cracking four hits in five at-bats against the St. Louis Browns, including a home run. Three of the hits were off right-hander Bob Harris and the fourth was off Jack Kramer, another right-hander.

On July 16, the Yankees began a series against the Indians in Cleveland. DiMaggio marked the occasion by reaching a pair of left-handers, Al Milnar and Joe Krakauskas, for three hits, one of them a double, in four times at the plate. Joe's streak now had run fifty-six games.

It ended the next night, July 17, before a crowd of 67,468 at Cleveland's Municipal Stadium. At that time it was the largest crowd ever to see a night game. The attraction was Joe DiMaggio. Fans all over the country, regardless of their fan affiliation, were pulling for Joe to keep his streak alive. The large crowd at Municipal Stadium that night of July 17, 1941, roared for DiMaggio to hit safely even as they rooted for a victory by the Indians.

Cleveland started a left-hander named Al Smith. In his first time at bat DiMaggio ripped a line drive toward third base. Kenny Keltner, the Indians' twenty-six-year-old third baseman, made a great backhanded stop and threw Joe out at first base.

Smith still was on the mound for the Indians when DiMaggio batted again in the top of the fourth. This time he received a base on balls. In the seventh inning, with the crowd beginning to grow anxious, Joe faced Smith a third time. As he had in the first inning, DiMaggio lined a rocket over third base. Again, Keltner made a miraculous backhanded stop to get Joe at first. The same Keltner would end the 1941 season with the highest fielding average among all American League third basemen.

There was one last chance for Joe. He came to bat in the eighth inning with the bases loaded. On the mound for Cleveland was a right-hander named Jim Bagby, Jr., son of the former Indian pitching star who won thirty-one games for the 1920 world champion Tribe.

DiMaggio lashed a ground ball towards short. "I hit it as hard as I ever hit any ground ball," Joe later recalled. Lou Boudreau, the Indians' fine shortstop, moved swiftly to his left. Boudreau was in front of the ball when it took a bad hop, but he speared it off his shoulder and flipped to second baseman Ray Mack, and Mack threw on to first to complete a double play.

"If I hadn't reacted quickly," Boudreau said later, "the ball probably would have gone over my head for a hit." But the ball didn't go over Boudreau's head and it was not a hit. It was an out. After sixty-three days, the incredible streak was over. The Indians, the last team to hold DiMaggio hitless before the streak, finally snapped it.

In the fifty-six games Joe batted .408 with ninety-one hits in two hundred twenty-three times at bat. Fifteen of the hits were home runs and DiMaggio drove in fifty-five runs in the fifty-six games. Over the same span, the Yankees won forty-one games and lost only thirteen. (Two other games ended in ties). This was a .759 pace. When the streak began the Yankees were in fourth place. When the streak ended the Yankees were in first place by six games, and they went on to clinch the pennant on the earliest clinching date in history, September 4. Their final margin over second-place Boston was a whopping seventeen games. Then the Yanks beat the Brooklyn Dodgers, four games to one, in the World Series.

Reflecting on his record afterward, DiMaggio said, "The thing I'm proudest of is that every base hit during the streak was honest. But I was sad it had to end. Strangely enough, despite all the pressure, I wanted to keep on going. I felt a little downhearted that I was stopped, but I got over it right away. It was like going into the seventh game of the World Series and losing it. That's how I felt. But I did want to keep on going. I wanted it to go on forever."

The next day Joe began another streak. This one reached sixteen games before he finally was stopped to complete the greatest half-season of hitting in major league baseball history.

The year 1941 was a great one in sports. Joe Louis outlasted Billy Conn in their heavyweight boxing title match. Whirlaway won the Triple Crown of horse racing. Lefty Grove won his three-hundredth game, Bob Feller won twenty-five for Cleveland, and Brooklyn Dodger rookie Pete Reiser became the youngest player ever to win the National League batting championship.

There was another remarkable batting accomplishment in 1941: Ted Williams of the Boston Red Sox won the American League batting crown with a .406 average. DiMaggio's final mark of .357 was good for third place. No one since Williams has compiled a .400 average for one full major league season, and perhaps no one ever will again.

But, more than anything else, 1941 belonged to Joe DiMaggio.

Joe DiMaggio's 56-Game Hitting Streak

Date—1941. Opp. Pitcher and Club.	AB	R	H	2B	3B	HR	RBI
May 15—Smith, Chicago	4	0	1	0	0	0	0
16—Lee, Chicago	4	2	2	0	1	1	1
17—Rigney, Chicago	3	1	1	0	0	0	0
18—Harris (2), Niggeling (1), St. Louis	3	3	3	1	0	0	1
19—Galehouse, St. Louis	3	0	1	1	0	0	0
20—Auker, St. Louis	5	1	1	0	0	0	1
21—Rowe (1), Benton (1), Detroit	5	0	2	0	0	0	1
22—McKain, Detroit	4	0	1	0	0	0	1
23—Newsome, Boston	5	0	1	0	0	0	2
24—Johnson, Boston	4	2	1	0	0	0	0
25—Grove, Boston	4	0	1	0	0	0	0
27—Chase (1), Anderson (2), Carrasquel (1), Washington	5	3	4	0	0	1	3
28—Hudson, Washington (Night)	4	1	1	0	1	0	0
29—Sundra, Washington	3	1	1	0	0	0	0
30—Johnson, Boston	2	1	1	0	0	0	0
30—Harris, Boston	3	0	1	1	0	0	0
16 games in May							
June 1—Milnar, Cleveland	4	1	1	0	0	0	0
1—Harder, Cleveland	4	0	1	0	0	0	0
2—Feller, Cleveland	4	2	2	1	0	0	0
3—Trout, Detroit	4	1	1	0	0	1	1
5—Newhouse, Detroit	5	1	1	0	0	1	1
7—Muncrief (1), Allen (1), Caster (1), St. Louis	5	2	3	0	0	0	1
8—Auker, St. Louis	4	3	2	0	0	2	4
8—Caster (1), Kramer (1), St. Louis	4	1	2	1	0	1	3
10—Rigney, Chicago	5	1	1	0	0	0	0
12—Lee, Chicago (Night)	4	1	2	0	0	1	1
14—Feller, Cleveland	2	0	1	1	0	0	1
15—Bagby, Cleveland	3	1	1	0	0	1	1
16—Milnar, Cleveland	5	0	1	1	0	0	0
17—Rigney, Chicago	4	1	1	0	0	0	0
18—Lee, Chicago	3	0	1	0	0	0	0
19—Smith (1), Ross (2), Chicago	3	2	3	0	0	1	2
20—Newsom (2), McKain (2), Detroit	5	3	4	1	0	0	1
21—Trout, Detroit	4	0	1	0	0	0	1
22—Newhouser (1), Newsom (1), Detroit	5	1	2	1	0	1	2
24—Muncrief, St. Louis	4	1	1	0	0	0	0
25—Galehouse, St. Louis	4	1	1	0	0	1	3
26—Auker, St. Louis	4	0	1	1	0	0	1
27—Dean, Philadelphia	3	1	2	0	0	1	2
28—Babich (1), Harris (1), Philadelphia	5	1	2	1	0	0	0
29—Leonard, Washington	4	1	1	1	0	0	0
29—Anderson, Washington	5	1	1	0	0	0	1
26 games in June							
July 1—Harris (1), Ryba (1), Boston	4	0	2	0	0	0	1
1—Wilson, Boston	3	1	1	0	0	0	0
2—Newsome, Boston	5	1	1	0	0	1	3
5—Marchildon, Philadelphia	4	2	1	0	0	1	2
6—Babich (1), Hadley (3), Philadelphia	5	2	4	1	0	0	2
6—Knott, Philadelphia	4	0	2	0	1	0	2
10—Niggeling, St. Louis (Night)	2	0	1	0	0	0	0
11—Harris (3), Kramer (1), St. Louis	5	1	4	0	0	1	2
12—Auker (1), Muncrief (1), St. Louis	5	1	2	1	0	0	1
13—Lyons (2), Hallett (1), Chicago	4	2	3	0	0	0	0
13—Lee, Chicago	4	0	1	0	0	0	0
14—Rigney, Chicago	3	0	1	0	0	0	0
15—Smith, Chicago	4	1	2	1	0	0	2
16—Milnar (2), Krakauskas (1), Cleveland	4	3	3	0	0	0	0
14 games in July							
Totals for 56 Games .408 Pct.	223	56	91	16	4	15	55

Stopped July 17 at Cleveland, night game, New York won, 4 to 3. First inning, Al Smith pitching, thrown out by Keltner; fourth inning, Smith pitching, received base on balls; seventh inning, Smith pitching, thrown out by Keltner; eighth inning, Jim Bagby, Jr., pitching, grounded into double play.

Jackie Robinson's Major League Debut

The announcement was simple. On the morning of April 9, 1947, reporters covering the Brooklyn Dodgers received, before an exhibition game, a single sheet of paper containing one sentence. The sentence read: "Brooklyn announces the purchase of the contract of Jack Roosevelt Robinson from Montreal. Signed, Branch Rickey."

The announcement marked the culmination of a two-year search by Rickey, who ran the Dodger ballclub, for the "right" man to break the unwritten, but strictly adhered to, law against blacks in organized baseball. To modern fans, the thought that only a quarter-century ago most black ballplayers had to be content with careers in the loosely organized Negro leagues, outside the umbrella of regular baseball government, seems staggering.

When Danny Murtaugh, manager of the Pittsburgh Pirates, handed to the umpires a lineup card that contained the names of nine black players on September 1, 1971, the news caused not a ripple. Blacks have achieved a major status in baseball—in all of major professional sports in the United States—since the day in 1945 when Rickey, the president and general manager of the Brooklyn team, first heard of a slugging infielder with the Kansas City Monarchs named Jackie Robinson.

The Monarchs were a Negro League team. Though he then was twenty-six years of age, Robinson could aspire to no better level of competition even though he had been heralded as the nation's finest all-round athlete while attending the University of California at Los Angeles a few scant years before. Jackie played baseball at UCLA but, strangely enough, that was his weakest sport in college. Robinson was a national record holder in the long jump event in track, a superb halfback for the UCLA football team, and one of the Pacific Coast's highest scorers in basketball.

But, largely because he was unable to enter other fields, Robinson embarked on a belated career in baseball's black leagues in the middle nineteen-forties after playing minor league pro football on the west coast for a time. Meanwhile in Brooklyn, Rickey, who long had rebelled at the unwritten barrier against blacks in baseball, was determined to find an athlete who would break it. He sent his scouts searching all over North America for black ballplayers who would qualify. Physical ability was not the only consideration.

"The first Negro in organized baseball had to be a great player, certainly," Rickey recalled years later. "But he also had to be a man of great character. He had to be a man who wouldn't fight back every time someone said something derogatory. After we discovered Jackie Robinson we spoke with him at length many times before coming to the conclusion that he was the ideal choice."

One early conversation between Rickey and Robinson has become classic over the years. The Dodger boss asked Jackie if, in the face of taunts from players and fans, he could turn his cheek. Robinson's answer was, "Mister Rickey, I've got another cheek."

Though Rickey felt Robinson could earn a spot on the Brooklyn team in 1946, he elected to have Jackie serve a one-year apprenticeship with the Dodgers' International League farm team in Montreal. Montreal was a fine choice for the debut of the first black in modern professional baseball. The racial issue in Canada was not nearly as heated as it was in the United States. Jackie thrived in the French-Canadian city in 1946, batting .349 and leading all International League second basemen in fielding average. Because of Robinson's presence in the lineup, the Montreal club received more attention from the press than almost every major league team that summer of '46. Jackie withstood the pressure of constant public scrutiny and revealed that he was ready to blaze the trail Branch Rickey had laid out for him.

The color barrier in baseball was constructed gradually. As far back as 1872, only three years after the Cincinnati Red Stockings, baseball's first professionals, began touring the country in search of competition, a black infielder named Bud Fowler played with an otherwise all-white team at New Castle, Pennsylvania. Appropriately, Fowler hailed from Cooperstown, N.Y., later baseball's shrine.

In the 1880s, the Walker brothers of Ohio, Moses Fleetwood, a catcher, and Weldy Wilberforce, an outfielder, played for Toledo in the American Association, when both the city and the league were in the major leagues. The Walkers were the first blacks to appear in major league baseball. But there were others, and blacks likely would have thrived in the sport, as they did in others, were it not for the stubborn racism of Adrian "Cap" Anson, the manager and leading player of the Chicago White Stockings of the late 1800s.

One of the premier first basemen of all time and duly enshrined in the Hall of Fame, Anson was at the forefront of a move to eliminate blacks from organized baseball, refusing to allow teams managed by him to take the field against clubs that included Negroes on their rosters. After years of following Anson's lead, other baseball clubs in other cities around the country continued to do so after Anson retired rather than embrace a new policy toward black players.

Major league baseball was not a concern of young Jackie Robinson, who had other problems to contend with. Born in Cairo, Georgia, on January 31, 1919, he moved with his mother and her four other children to Pasadena, California, in 1920 after the father deserted the family. Mrs. Robinson and her brood moved into a home on Pepper Street, a poor area of Pasadena populated mostly by Mexicans, Japanese, and Negroes. In order to keep food on the table, Mrs. Robinson worked long hours uncomplainingly as a domestic servant.

Two of the Robinson boys became great athletes— Jackie and his older brother Mack. The latter specialized in track and became such a great sprinter that he finished a close second to Jesse Owens in the 200-meter dash at the 1936 Berlin Olympics.

Jackie looked forward to putting his athletic skills to use as a physical education instructor and as a coach. After serving in the Army, where he reached the rank of first lieutenant, Jackie did coach basketball for a time at Samuel Houston College, a small Negro school in Austin, Texas. This was shortly before he joined the Kansas City Monarchs as a shortstop for $400 a month.

It was while playing for Kansas City that he first was spotted by a black sportswriter named Wendell Smith, then sports editor of the *Pittsburgh Courier,* one of the nation's largest papers specializing in news by, for, and about black people. Smith was a close friend of Rickey and many baseball scouts and, aware of Rickey's search for a player to break the major league color barrier, advised him and his scouts of Robinson's presence.

Though Rickey intended to bring Jackie to the Dodgers for the 1947 season, he persuaded Robinson to spend spring training that year with the Montreal club, known as the Royals. That way, the Dodger president reasoned, Jackie wouldn't be constantly pursued by the press, and the potentially hostile fans in the southern cities, where exhibition games mostly are played, wouldn't be able to abuse him.

Two days after Robinson's contract was purchased by Brooklyn, he appeared in his first game in Dodger uniform number 42, the number which he was to carry throughout his decade with the team. It was an exhibition game against the New York Yankees, played before 24,237 fans at Ebbets Field. The Dodgers routed the Yankees, 14-6, but Jackie was unable to hit safely. He did drive in three runs, however, with two long flyballs and an infield out. Playing first base, Robinson handled the position flawlessly. Though Jackie was really better suited to play second base or shortstop, the Dodgers already were fortified at those positions with Eddie Stanky at second and Peewee Reese at short.

It would be another year before Robinson became the Dodger second baseman, following Stanky's trade to Boston. Jackie played several seasons at second, and later became a Brooklyn regular at third base and in leftfield. He never minded switching positions if he felt it would help the club. That's why Jackie, informed that the Dodgers had a depth problem at first base in 1947, agreed to handle that job.

His official major league debut in a regular season game came against the Boston Braves on Tuesday afternoon, April 15, 1947. It was not one of the most auspicious of debuts. "I did a miserable job," Robinson recalled many years afterward. "There was an overflow crowd at Ebbets Field. If they expected any miracles out of me, they were sadly disappointed."

Facing Boston right-hander Johnny Sain four times, Robinson failed to hit safely in his first major league game. He grounded out to third, flied to leftfield, bounced into a double play, and was safe on an error in the seventh inning. After reaching base, Jackie scored what proved to be the winning run in a 5-3 Brooklyn triumph.

For three innings Sain and Joe Hatten of the Dodgers pitched hitless ball. Brooklyn broke through in the bottom of the fourth when centerfielder Pete Reiser walked and eventually scored from third on an infield out by Bruce Edwards, the catcher.

After tying the score in the top of the fifth, the Braves went ahead with two runs in the sixth. Brooklyn reduced Boston's lead to 3-2 in the bottom of the sixth.

In the bottom of the seventh, the Dodgers rallied to win the game. Second baseman Eddie Stanky started the rally with a walk. Robinson, batting second in the order, was next up. Jackie later admitted he had a lot of trouble with Sain, the Braves' hurler, that day. "All I saw from him were curveballs," Robinson recalled. "Curves of different sizes, shapes and speeds, and I wondered whether maybe I'd soon be back in Montreal."

With Stanky on first in the bottom of the seventh, Jackie attempted to sacrifice him to second. Earl Torgeson, Boston's bespectacled first baseman, charged Robinson's bunt but, attempting to throw to the second baseman covering first, hit Robinson in the shoulder with the ball and it bounded into rightfield. Jackie ended up at second base and Stanky at third. A long double by Reiser against the screen in rightfield scored both men. Later in the inning a ground ball by third baseman Spider Jorgensen delivered Reiser with the fifth Brooklyn run. Howie "Stretch" Schultz, a six-foot, seven-inch player, took over the first base chores as a defensive replacement for the Dodgers for the final two innings. Robinson, remember, still was a newcomer to the position.

Though it wasn't an outstanding first game in the majors Jackie wasn't disheartened. He got his first hit the next day against Boston southpaw Glenn Elliott and his first home run the day after that off Giant lefthander Dave Koslo at the Polo Grounds.

Robinson went on to bat .297 for Brooklyn that first year. Two years later, in 1949, he reached his one-season high of .342 and won the National League batting championship. For 10 years with the Dodgers his lifetime batting average was a robust .311. But his legacy only begins with the lines of small type in the record books.

Jackie Robinson died early the morning of October 24, 1972, a Tuesday, at his home in Stamford, Connecticut. The cause of death was diagnosed as a heart attack brought on by complications of diabetes, the blood disease that had ravaged the once magnificent body for some years and had reduced Jackie to near blindness and a far older appearance than his chronological age, fifty-three. Only a few short weeks after Jackie's passing, Wendell Smith, the sportswriter who had praised Robinson to Branch Rickey in 1945, also died, of cancer. He had written often and glowingly of Jackie over the years, and had become a close friend of the entire Robinson family.

So the man who lived the story and the man who wrote it both were gone. But in all the years of major league sports still to come, the contribution of Jack Roosevelt Robinson never will be forgotten. He had the courage to face an uncertain situation when he might have followed the lead of many others and taken the easy way out.

Controversial because of the forceful manner in which he championed the cause of black athletes in his later years, Robinson's last public words were typical of him. At one of the games of the 1972 World Series, Jackie threw out the first ball and told a crowd at Cincinnati's Riverfront Stadium and a television audience of millions, "I won't be satisfied until I look over at the third base coaching box and see a black man there as manager."

Robinson didn't live to see a black manager in baseball, but the trail Jackie blazed on the diamond would make it a lot smoother for the man who someday would get the call as a pioneer black manager. Clearly, Robinson's influence on the history of baseball would be felt for many more years to come.

Tuesday, April 15, 1947, at Ebbets Field, Brooklyn, N.Y.

Boston	AB.	R.	H.	Brooklyn	AB.	R.	H.
Culler, ss	3	0	0	Stanky, 2b	3	1	0
Sisti, ss	0	0	0	ROBINSON, 1b	3	1	0
Hopp, cf	5	0	1	Schultz, 1b	0	0	0
McCormick, rf	4	0	3	Reiser, cf	2	3	2
Elliott, 3b	2	0	1	Walker, rf	3	0	1
Litwhiler, lf	3	1	0	Tatum, rf	0	0	0
Rowell, lf	1	0	0	Furillo, rf	0	0	0
Torgeson, 1b	4	1	0	Hermanski, lf	4	0	1
Masi, c	3	0	0	Edwards, c	2	0	0
Ryan, 2b	4	1	3	aRackley	0	0	0
Sain, p	1	0	0	Bragan, c	1	0	0
Cooper, p	0	0	0	Jorgensen, 3b	3	0	0
dNeill	0	0	0	Reese, ss	3	0	1
Lanfranconi, p	0	0	0	Hatten, p	2	0	1
eHolmes	1	0	0	Gregg, p	1	0	0
	—	—	—	Casey, p	0	0	0
Totals	31	3	8	bStevens	1	0	0
				cVaughn	1	0	0
					—	—	—
				Totals	29	5	6

aRan for Edwards in sixth
bStruck out for Hatten in sixth
cGrounded out for Tatum in seventh
dHit by pitch for Cooper in eighth
eFlied out for Culler in eighth

Boston .... 0 0 0 0 1 2 0 0 0—3
Brooklyn .... 0 0 0 1 0 1 3 0 x—5

Error—Edwards, Torgeson. Runs batted in—Edwards, Jorgensen, Hermanski, Reiser 2, Hopp, Ryan 2. Two-base hits—Reese, Reiser. Sacrifice hits—Sain 2, Culler, Masi, Hermanski. Left on bases—Boston 12, Brooklyn 7. Double play—Stanky, Reese and Robinson; Culler, Ryan and Torgeson. Bases on balls—Hatten 3, Sain 5, Gregg 2. Struck out—Hatten 2, Sain 1, Gregg 2, Lanfranconi 2, Casey 1. Hits off—Sain 6 in 6 innings (faced five batters in seventh), Cooper 0 in 1, Lanfranconi 0 in 1; Hatten 6 in 6, Gregg 2 in 2 1/3, Casey 0 in 2/3. Wild pitch—Hatten. Hit batsmen—Edwards (by Sain), Litwhiler (by Hatten), Neale (by Gregg). Winning pitcher—Gregg. Losing pitcher—Sain. Umpires—Pinelli, Barlick, Gore. Attendance—25,623.

Bobby Thomson—The Most Dramatic Homer

If Boston's National League team of 1914 qualified to be called the "Miracle Braves," what term would be suitable to describe the New York Giants of 1951?

On July 4, 1914, the Braves were mired in last place in the National League. Yet manager George Stallings rallied his men, and the Braves stormed to the pennant and then won the World Series in a four-game sweep over the heavily favored Philadelphia Athletics. So swift was the Braves' surge to the top that by August 11, 1914, they were only three and one-half games out of first place.

On the Fourth of July in 1951, the New York Giants trailed the Brooklyn Dodgers, who were running away with the National League pennant race. On August 11, 1951, at the same point in the schedule from which the Braves had made their final climb to the top thirty-seven years before, the Giants still were far behind the first-place Dodgers. The Giants were in second place but a distant thirteen and one-half lengths behind. With only forty-four games remaining on the schedule, there seemed no possible way for the Giants to make up the lost ground.

The favorites of the Polo Grounds promptly ran off a winning streak of sixteen games, slicing the Dodger lead to five games. Earlier in the season the same Giants lost eleven straight, sending fiery manager Leo Durocher into a frenzy.

Now it was a chastened Durocher manipulating the Giant strings during the stretch drive. Leo didn't shout or berate his players, but sat calmly on the bench each day, emitting silent prayers that the Giants' streak was not coming too late. In the last six weeks of the season, Durocher, notorious for bawling out his players in frequently called clubhouse meetings, did not call one clubhouse meeting. No meetings were necessary. The Giant players knew they had to win practically every game they played during those final six weeks. And they came as close to realizing that goal as could have been considered possible. Of their final forty-four games, the Giants won thirty-seven, an astonishing victory rate of .841.

The Dodgers aided the New York cause by losing several key games in the closing weeks. On the last morning of the regular season the two clubs were tied for first place. Larry Jansen, who already had won twenty-one games for the Giants, pitched his team's final game in Boston, and when he won it, 3-2, the Giants took sole command of first place. Everything now depended upon the result of the Dodgers' final game, being played at Philadelphia.

The Dodgers and Phillies battled into extra innings with the score tied, 8-8. The Brooklyn players already knew the result of the Giant game. Now they had to win their game to force a playoff for the pennant. Jackie Robinson, giving one of the finest clutch performances any player ever has given, came to the rescue of the Dodgers. In the twelfth inning, with the bases loaded, Eddie Waitkus, the Phillies' first baseman, ripped a hard smash that seemed ticketed for the outfield. If the ball went through, the Giants were champions of the National League.

But Robinson raced to his left and made an impossible diving catch of Waitkus' low liner inches above the ground. His desperate catch jarred the Brooklyn second baseman. He fell hard on his shoulder and collapsed. It was several minutes before he was able to rise shakily and walk uncertainly back to the dugout.

The game continued to the fourteenth inning. The first two Dodgers were easy outs at the hands of Robin Roberts, the Phillies' ace. Then Robinson stepped up, still reeling slightly from the force of his fall in catching Waitkus' line drive. Roberts got a ball and a strike on Robinson. Jackie walloped the next pitch into the upper leftfield stands to give Brooklyn a 9-8 lead.

Bud Podbielan was pitching in relief for the Dodgers. In the bottom of the fourteenth he surrendered a lead-off single to Richie Ashnurn, who then was sacrificed to second base. Bearing down, Podbielan got the powerful Del Ennis on a routine fly ball. Then it was Waitkus' turn again. This time he lifted an easy fly to left. Andy Pafko squeezed it for the final out and the Dodgers, who seemed to have the pennant wrapped up six weeks earlier, had just barely escaped the regular season with a tie.

The Giants followed the final innings of the Dodger-Phillie game while they were en route back to New York by train after their game in Boston. The train in which the Giants rode was one of the first to have regular telephone service, and inning-by-inning scores from Philadelphia were relayed to the anxious Giants. The team management ordered champagne and other festive trimmings be set up in the dining car should news of a Dodger defeat come from Philadelphia.

When the news came that Robinson had hit a dramatic fourteenth-inning home run and that the Dodgers had won, the Giants sat stunned. One voice finally broke the silence of the players in the railroad car. Speaking to Jim Hearn, who had been tapped by manager Leo Durocher to start the first playoff game the next day—now that a playoff series was necessary—

the voice cried, "Okay, Jim, you'll get 'em tomorrow." The voice belonged to Bobby Thomson.

One of the few players in the major leagues who was born in the British Isles, Robert Brown Thomson first saw the light of day in Glasgow, Scotland, on October 25, 1923. But Bobby spent much of his early life in his adopted home of New York, on Staten Island. This resulted in his being labeled "The Staten Island Scot" when he reached the big leagues of baseball years later.

Thomson, a right-handed batter and thrower, was a good minor league hitter, though he couldn't seem to decide whether he preferred playing in the infield or in the outfield. He divided his time pretty evenly between the outfield and third base, and when he made it to the Giants for an eighteen-game whirl in 1946, he was listed as a combination infielder-outfielder.

In 1947, Bobby was one of the regular Giant outfielders, except for nine appearances at second base. For the Scottish-born young man, his first full season of major league ball was a promising one. Thomson fitted right in with the rest of the 1947 Giants, one of the most powerful slugging teams of all time. The Giants bombed 221 home runs to establish a major league record for one year. Johnny Mize, the first baseman, belted fifty-one roundtrippers; outfielder Willard Marshall hit thirty-six, catcher Walker Cooper hit thirty-five and Thomson hit twenty-nine. As a team, New York had sixty-five more homers than any other National League club in 1947.

Unfortunately, despite their lusty hitting, the Giants didn't have pitching to match. Their combined earned-run average of 4.44 was seventh best in the eight-team league, and New York finished the 1947 season in fourth place, thirteen games behind pennant-winning Brooklyn.

The Giants were sliding into the second division

when Leo Durocher replaced Mel Ott as manager after sixty-five games of the 1948 season. "Leo the Lip" had begun 1948 as field boss of the arch-rival Dodgers, and his defection to the Giants sent shock waves throughout the baseball world. Durocher had long been identified with Brooklyn baseball, and had managed the 1941 Dodgers to the National League flag.

Durocher's arrival also sent sparks flying throughout the Giant lineup. Leo recognized that he had a powerful hitting array. He also recognized that, with the exception of Bobby Thomson, none of his sluggers could run very well. Durocher beseeched the club owner, Horace Stoneham, to pull a series of trades that would guarantee Leo "my kind of team," a team with speed and hustle. In the ensuing one and one-half seasons, Mize, Marshall and Cooper, three of the big four power hitters of the 1947 Giants, were sent off to other teams.

Thomson, a lithe 6-2, 180-pounder, remained and grew in acclaim as one of the Giants' most steady and proficient performers. After slipping to sixteen home runs in 1948, Bobby climbed to twenty-seven homers in 1949 and added another twenty-five in 1950. Going into the 1951 campaign, Bobby was an established major league veteran at age twenty-seven.

Meanwhile, Durocher was building his kind of team. From the Braves he obtained the heart of a new infield, second baseman Eddie Stanky and shortstop Alvin Dark. He brought in the Giants' first two black players, Monte Irvin, an outfielder, and Hank Thompson, who played all over the diamond. The Giants also obtained a pitcher named Jim Hearn on waivers from the Cardinals, and took a chance on a thirty-three-year-old right-hander named Sal Maglie, who had been a consistent losing pitcher in the minor leagues. Also about this time Leo looked after the signing of a nineteen-year-old baseball prodigy from Alabama named Willie Mays.

All these players made significant contributions to the Giants' stirring stretch drive in the last six weeks of the 1951 season. Durocher's kind of players were playing the way he wanted them to play, and that's all he asked.

There were others too, of course. The ranking ace of the pitching staff was Larry Jansen, a right-hander who had one of his finest years. The right-fielder was a slap-hitter named Don Mueller, whose control of the bat earned him the nickname of "Mandrake the Magician." Whitey Lockman, another aggressive line-drive hitter with fair power, opened the season in leftfield, but later was moved to first base as Monte Irvin took over leftfield. Irvin went on to lead the National League in runs batted in.

The catcher was Wes Westrum, a fine handler of pitchers and a power hitter despite a low batting average. He received a lot of credit for his work with the Giants' three-man starting rotation of Jansen, Maglie and Hearn. These three formed the nucleus of the New York staff that concluded the 1951 season with the best team earned-run average in the league.

The Dodgers of 1951 were the epitome of the power-hitting team. They led all sixteen teams in the major leagues in home runs and slugging average. Their line-up featured first baseman Gil Hodges, Robinson at second, Duke Snider in centerfield, Carl Furillo in right-field and Roy Campanella behind the plate.

Brooklyn's pitching was not on a par with the Giants, but with all their hitting, the Dodgers got by with slightly less pitching than other teams. Still Brooklyn had big Don Newcombe, equally big Ralph Branca and a host of other capable veterans. The Giant-Dodger playoff matchup seemed very even.

If either team could point to an edge after the 154-game regular schedule, the Dodgers could call on the relative ease with which they had handled the Giants during the year. In their first fifteen meetings of the campaign, the Dodgers won twelve.

But past history had no meaning now. As the Dodgers and Giants squared off in their playoff series to determine the National League champion, each team had ninety-six victories and fifty-eight defeats. The first team to win two more games would become champion.

The regular season ended on Sunday, and the playoffs began the very next day. The first game was played at Ebbets Field in Brooklyn. Durocher called on Hearn to pitch for the Giants. Chuck Dressen, the Dodger manager, gave the crucial starting assignment to Ralph Branca.

Known as "Hawk" because of his elongated nose, Ralph Theodore Joseph Branca was practically a local New York boy who made good with the Dodgers. Born on January 6, 1926, Branca grew up in Mount Vernon, a few miles north of New York City in Westchester County. Ralph grew up well. By the time he reached the Dodgers in 1944 when he was just eighteen, Branca stood six feet, three inches tall and weighed well over two hundred pounds.

Ralph had brief flings in Brooklyn for three years, but wasn't really ready for the majors until 1947, when he was twenty-one. That year Branca won a game for every one of his years on earth. His twenty-one victories against only twelve defeats carried the Dodgers to the National League pennant.

Ralph slipped slightly after that early peak, but still was a valuable and knowledgeable pitcher for Brooklyn in following seasons. Branca had real intelligence. He was college-educated, at New York University, and the future would hold a prosperous career as an insurance executive for him.

But in the National League pennant playoffs of 1951, Ralph still was three months away from his twenty-sixth birthday and the future seemed a long way off.

Though Brooklyn held the home field advantage for the opening playoff game, the Dodgers couldn't capitalize. Hearn smothered the Dodger sluggers, and the only homer of the day was struck by Bobby Thomson, a two-run blow, his thirty-first circuit drive of the year. The Giants won, 3-1, and Brooklyn lost more than the game. Campanella injured his leg and was out for the remainder of the playoffs. This didn't augur well for the Dodgers as the scene shifted to the Polo Grounds for the second playoff game. If a third game were necessary, it also would be played at the Polo Grounds.

A third game, it was obvious early, would be necessary. Both managers, Durocher and Dressen, took calculated risks in assigning their starting pitchers for the second playoff game. Each of them named hurlers they had customarily used in relief situations. The Giant starter was Sheldon Jones. For the Dodgers, it was Clem Labine. Dressen's gamble paid off. Labine, a rookie, pitched a strong game, allowing only six hits and no runs. The big Dodger bats belted Jones out of the box early, and Brooklyn raced to an easy 10-0 triumph.

Now it was Wednesday, October 3. The Giants and Dodgers each had played one hundred and fifty-six games of baseball for the year. Each had won ninety-seven and lost fifty-nine. The magic number now was ninety-eight. The team that won its ninety-eighth game of 1951 on this day would be the champion of the National League.

Each team had a ready and rested pitching star to start this game. Brooklyn had Don Newcombe, winner of twenty games and loser of only nine during the year. New York had Sal Maglie, with an even better record of twenty-three victories and a mere six defeats. The game promised to be a pitching duel worthy of such a dramatic situation as a final playoff game. The weather, on the other hand, lacked the appeal of the game situation. The day came up overcast, and rain could be seen lurking behind the dark clouds. When the game got under way in early afternoon, there were, surprisingly, many empty seats in the Polo Grounds, where 34,320 fans were assembled for what figured to be one of the most dramatic baseball games ever played.

Maglie showed signs of weakness in the first inning, which usually was his poorest inning. He had trouble locating the plate and walked both Peewee Reese and Snider. Then Robinson lined a single to leftfield to score Reese. The Dodgers led, 1-0, and there was only one out with two Brooklyn runners on base. However, Maglie closed the door on further Dodger scoring in the first.

The Giants threatened against Newcombe in the second. Lockman singled. Thomson was next up. He was playing third base this game, and in fact, had played a lot of third base in 1951 as Durocher shuffled lineups constantly. Bobby lined a hit into left. Believing he could stretch the hit into a double, he rounded first and charged toward second with his head down.

Surprise! Lockman had stopped at second after Thomson's hit. Bobby tried to wheel back to first base, but was run down and tagged out by the alert Brooklyn infield. It was not a great beginning to Bobby Thomson's day.

The score remained 1-0 in favor of the Dodgers as the game entered its middle innings. Dusk settled over the stadium early in the fall afternoon, and the Polo Grounds' lights came on in the fifth inning. "Now maybe Thomson will be able to see where he's running," one quipster observed.

After keeping their fans suffering for six scoreless innings, the Giants tied the score at 1-1 in the seventh. Thomson, gaining some measure of redemption for his second-inning baserunning boner, drove in the run for New York with a fly ball. Irvin opened the Giant seventh with a double and moved to third on Lockman's sacrifice bunt. Then Irvin came across home plate as Thomson flied out.

The 1-1 tie didn't last very long. Reese spanked a single to right as the Dodgers started working on Maglie in the top of the eighth inning. Snider sent Reese to third with another single. Attempting to pitch carefully to the dangerous Jackie Robinson, Maglie threw a curveball into the dirt. It eluded Westrum and skipped past to the screen behind home plate. Reese scored on the wild pitch. Robinson finally waited out a walk.

Pafko, the next batter for Brooklyn, pulled the ball down the third base line. Thomson tried to backhand it, but it bounced off his glove for a base hit, scoring Snider. After Hodges was retired, Billy Cox, the Dodgers' third baseman, hit a sharp grounder to Thomson, the Giants' third baseman. Bobby positioned himself in front of the ball, but it took a sudden skip, caromed off his shoulder and continued bouncing into leftfield. Robinson scored the third Dodger run of the inning, and the visiting team led, 4-1. Thomson received a chorus of boos from the Giant fans, who were now fearful that New York's pennant chances were slipping away.

Newcombe set the Giants down in the bottom of the eighth and Larry Jansen went to the mound for the Giants in the top of the ninth. Maglie had been removed for a pinch hitter when New York took its turn at the plate in the eighth.

Jansen retired the Dodgers, and it still was a 4-1 game as the last half of the ninth began. The Giants' cause appeared hopeless now, with Newcombe pitching strongly in protection of his three-run lead. But Durocher, who had seen his team overcome supposedly insurmountable odds to merely reach these playoffs, implored his men to stage one more miracle.

Alvin Dark was first up for the Giants in the bottom of the ninth. Newcombe poured over two quick strikes. But then New York's shortstop punched a single to rightfield. Mueller, who sprayed his hits all over the diamond, came up and placed the ball perfectly between first and second. The ball wasn't hit hard, but it got through to rightfield, just escaping Hodges' desperate lunge. Dark moved to third on the play.

The dangerous Irvin was up next. Monte had already driven home one hundred and twenty-one runs for 1951. Here was a golden chance to add to that total. A home run would tie the game. But Newcombe, finding a new source of strength, enticed Irvin into hitting a soft pop foul to Hodges for the first out.

Newcombe never got another out. Lockman whacked a solid double to left, scoring Dark. Racing to third on the play, Mueller slid and badly twisted his ankle. He had to be carried off the field on a stretcher, and Clint Hartung was sent to third base as a pinch runner.

The score now was 4-2, and Dodger manager Dressen was taking no more chances with the tying runs in scoring position. A new pitcher would have to come in to relieve Newcombe.

Two pitchers had been warming up in the Brooklyn bullpen—Carl Erskine and Ralph Branca, who had started and lost the first playoff game. Dressen got on the telephone in the dugout and asked his bullpen coach, "Who's ready out there?"

"Erskine just bounced a curveball," replied the coach. "Branca looks fast and loose."

"Send in Branca, then," replied Dressen.

When Ralph arrived at the mound Dressen handed him the ball. "Get him out," he instructed the big right-hander.

The "him" referred to by Dressen was Bobby Thomson, waiting at the plate. Before entering the batter's box and taking his customary spread stance, Bobby also conversed briefly with his manager, Durocher. "If you ever hit one now," Leo shrieked hoarsely, "hit one now." The manager's words had a settling effect on Thomson. Years later he recalled his reaction to Leo's advice:

"I could see Leo was as excited as I was and it calmed me down. Going up to the plate, I said to myself, 'You're a pro. Act like one. Do a good job.' I was concerned only with getting a hit and keeping the rally alive."

Bobby realized he had some making up to do for his earlier play in the third playoff game. But Branca was perfectly willing to make Thomson look bad again. They faced each other, pitcher and batter, both New York residents, each man concentrating with all his might.

Branca threw his first pitch to the plate. It was a low inside fastball. Lou Jorda, the home plate umpire, called it a strike.

Branca tried to get his second pitch high and inside so that Thomson, if he swung, could not connect solidly. Ralph checked the baserunners, Hartung at third, Lockman at second, kicked and threw.

The ball came in lower than Branca had wanted it

to be. Thomson swung and the ball soared toward the leftfields stands.

"Get down! Get down!" Billy Cox shrieked at the ball as it passed high over his head at third base and rose into deep leftfield. Pafko stationed himself against the wall and put his hands up, hoping the ball might fade and land in his glove.

But the ball didn't fade. It flew into the leftfield stands where a mob of deliriously happy Giant fans descended upon it as Pafko could only turn and stare helplessly. It was a three-run homer and the Giants had won the game, 5-4, and with it, the National League championship!

Gasping for breath in his excitement as he circled the bases to score behind Hartung and Lockman, Thomson received a hysterical welcome when he crossed the plate. "I didn't run around the bases," Bobby said later. "I rode around them on a cloud." Every member of the Giants and what seemed like half the spectators in the stands mobbed Thomson, everyone trying to embrace him at once.

Up in the broadcast booth of the Giants, announcer Russ Hodges succumbed to his emotions. At the top of his voice he told his radio audience the story again and again: "The Giants win the pennant! The Giants win the pennant! The Giants win the pennant! . . ."

Historians of world affairs have noted for posterity that on October 3, 1951, the Soviet Union exploded an atom bomb at a testing grounds.

But in New York and around the baseball world on that day, there was only one explosion: the one that sounded when Bobby Thomson's ninth-inning home run landed in the leftfield stands—the most dramatic home run ever hit.

Wednesday, October 3, 1951, at Polo Grounds, New York

Brooklyn	AB.	R.	H.	New York	AB.	R.	H.
Furillo, rf	5	0	0	Stanky, 2b	4	0	0
Reese, ss	4	2	1	Dark, ss	4	1	1
Snider, cf	3	1	2	Mueller, rf	4	0	1
Robinson, 2b	2	1	1	cHartung	0	1	0
Pafko, lf	4	0	1	Irvin, lf	4	1	1
Hodges, 1b	4	0	0	Lockman, 1b	3	1	2
Cox, 3b	4	0	2	THOMSON, 3b	4	1	3
Walker, c	4	0	1	Mays, cf	3	0	0
Newcombe, p	4	0	0	Westrum, c	0	0	0
Branca, p	0	0	0	aRigney	1	0	0
				Noble, c	0	0	0
Totals	34	4	8	Maglie, p	2	0	0
				bThompson	1	0	0
				Jansen, p	0	0	0
				Totals	30	5	8

*One out when winning run scored
aStruck out for Westrum in eighth
bGrounded out for Maglie in eighth
cRan for Mueller in ninth

```
Brooklyn ..........................1 0 0   0 0 0   0 3 0—4
New York ........................0 0 0   0 0 0   1 0 4—5
```

Runs batted in—Robinson, Thomson 4, Pafko, Cox, Lockman (Reese scored on Maglie wild pitch in eighth). Two base hits—Thomson, Irvin, Lockman. Home run—Thomson. Sacrifice—Lockman. Double plays—Cox, Robinson and Hodges; Reese, Robinson and Hodges. Left on base—Brooklyn 7, New York 3. Bases on balls off—Maglie 4, Newcombe 2. Struck out—by Maglie 6, Newcombe 2. Hits off—Maglie 8 in 8 innings, Jansen 0 in 1, Newcombe 7 in 8 1/3, Branca 1 in 0 (faced one batter in ninth). Winning pitcher—Jansen (23-11). Losing pitcher—Branca (13-12). Wild pitch—Maglie. Umpires—Jorda, Conlan, Stewart, Goetz. Time—2:28. Attendance—34,320.

The Greatest Slugging Day

The last day of July in 1954 came up one of the hottest and muggiest days in Brooklyn history. Early that Saturday afternoon the mercury soared to a reading of 95.3 degrees. The humidity level was almost as high. The Dodgers were playing a home game at Ebbets Field that day, but only 12,263 fans turned out at the ballpark. Presumably, the oppressive heat drove the Brooklyn faithful to cool their heels and other parts of their anatomy at the borough's famed beaches in the Brighton and Coney Island sections.

From a Brooklyn point of view, Dodger fans would have done well to offer a shady spot under a beach umbrella to Joe Adcock, the slugging first baseman of the Milwaukee Braves, who provided the opposition at Ebbets Field that afternoon.

The only thing hotter than the weather in Brooklyn on July 31, 1954, was Joe Adcock's bat. For it was on that day that the strapping right-handed hitter delivered four home runs and a double against the luckless Dodger pitching staff, the greatest one-day slugging feat in baseball history.

Joe, who stood six feet, four inches, and weighed two hundred and thirty-five pounds at the peak of his playing power, played seventeen years in the major leagues and clouted three hundred and thirty-six home runs, an impressive total but well below the "super-slugger" status two of his Milwaukee teammates of 1954 were to attain. Two of the young Braves in the team's second year in Milwaukee (they were the Boston Braves until 1953) were Eddie Mathews and Hank Aaron. Both these men were to compile more than five hundred home runs.

Yet for sheer power, few major leaguers ever have exceeded Adcock's physical strength. He hit two of the longest home runs on record. In 1953, he leveled on a pitch thrown by Jim Hearn of the New York Giants and hit it ten rows deep into the bleachers of the Polo Grounds, four hundred and sixty-five feet from home plate. It was the first time anyone ever had hammered a ball into the Polo Grounds bleachers. Only two other players managed the feat before the stadium was demolished more than a decade later. In 1962, Lou Brock and Hank Aaron powdered balls thrown by hapless pitchers of the New York Mets into the bleachers on successive days!

In 1956, Joe leaned into a pitch at Ebbets Field and sent it sailing over the roof. The ball cleared a barrier eighty-three feet high and three hundred and fifty feet away from the plate at ground level and landed in a parking lot across the street. It was calculated that the ball traveled five hundred feet before landing. No one ever had hit a ball over the Ebbets Field roof before. And no one after Adcock ever did again. The old Brooklyn park was torn down when the Dodgers moved to Los Angeles in 1958.

Joe must have been sorry to see Ebbets Field go. It was a park almost custom made for right-handed power hitters, and the hometown Dodgers had such hitters in abundance. The leftfield stands were a relatively close three hundred and fifty feet from home plate. Rival power hitters of the right-handed variety found the stands as inviting as did the Brooklyn sluggers like Gil Hodges, Roy Campanella and Jackie Robinson. Joe Adcock loved those stands. In fact, the very sight of Dodger pitching, at Ebbets Field or elsewhere, made

Joe's mouth water. In 1956, Adcock belted thirteen home runs against Brooklyn. No one ever has devastated an opposing team more than Joe devastated Brooklyn during the 1956 season.

And for one single day of devastation nothing ever has equaled Adcock's destruction of the Dodgers on that hot July 31 of 1954.

The Braves were riding high when they came into Ebbets Field for a four-game series against the Dodgers. They had won seven straight games. On Friday night, the first game in Brooklyn, the Braves ran their streak to eight in a row. Adcock helped the Milwaukee cause with a home run in the fourth inning. But later in the game he broke his bat. Adcock was hitting very well with that bat. His batting average was well over .300 and his home run and runs batted in totals also were among the highest in the National League. Joe really hated to lose that bat.

He had to borrow a new bat for the second game of the series on Saturday afternoon. He ended up with one that belonged to Charley White, a reserve catcher with the Braves. It wasn't the most suitable bat Joe could have found. "I don't know why I chose that bat," Adcock said later. "It was much heavier than the one I had been using, the heaviest on the team, in fact. I could hardly carry it up to the plate."

It might have been less painful for the Dodgers had Joe been unable to lug the heavy piece of lumber up to bat. At the very least, he could have dropped it on his toe.

Jim Wilson for Milwaukee and Don Newcombe for Brooklyn were the starting pitchers. Neither survived the second inning. Each side scored a single run in the first. But the Braves routed Newcombe in the second. Adcock touched off a three-run inning by belting a Newcombe fastball into the lower left-centerfield stands.

Though the Dodgers loaded the bases in the bottom of the second, forcing the removal from the mound of Wilson in favor of Lew Burdette, there was no Brooklyn scoring.

With Erv Palica pitching for the home team in the third, Adcock came to bat for the second time and lined a long double to leftfield. But Joe, though swinging a heavy bat in the heavy Brooklyn atmosphere, was just getting warmed up.

In the fifth inning, Palica still was pitching for Brooklyn. Adcock gave the Braves a 9-1 lead when he connected with a Palica slider and blasted it off the leftfield facade with two teammates on base.

Joe's next turn at bat came in the top of the seventh inning. A rookie right-hander named Pete Wojey was on the mound for the Dodgers. One Brave runner was on base and it quickly became clear that Adcock wasn't going to receive a good pitch to hit from Wojey.

"Dusty Boggess was the plate umpire," Joe recalled years later. "The first two pitches to me were very high for balls. Then Wojey threw a third ball. I said to myself 'I'm going to have a cut at the next one, wherever it is.' It was a curveball, and it came in at eye level. There's no doubt it would have been the fourth ball. But I swung and darned if it didn't end up in the lower leftfield stands, almost exactly where I hit the first one off Newcombe. It was a lucky swing, but I always said when I was playing ball that I'd rather be lucky than good."

Joseph Wilbur Adcock always considered himself lucky, from his first recollections of life on his father's farm in the little town of Coushatta, about fifty miles southeast of Shreveport in western Louisiana. Coushatta had a population of about four hundred citizens when Joe was born there on October 30, 1927. When he returned to the farm to raise thoroughbred horses after his days in baseball were done, Coushatta had a population of nearly two thousand five hundred.

"All the contacts I made in baseball helped me get started in the business of raising horses," Adcock pointed out one afternoon at the farm in Coushatta. "It was very fortunate that I got into sports, and very fortunate that many good opportunities came my way because of sports."

Basketball was the big sport in Joe Adcock's youth, and he became known as one of the finest cagers in Louisiana's Red River County. When he graduated from high school, Joe received an athletic scholarship to attend Louisiana State University in Baton Rouge.

During Joe's days at LSU, the Bengals were one of the strongest teams in Southeastern Conference basketball. In the season of 1945-46, LSU won the conference championship, sweeping all eight league games and winning fifteen of seventeen games overall. Adcock, then known as "Joe Bill Adcock," was the leading scorer in conference games for the Bengals. He tallied seventy-four points, including a one-game record haul of thirty-one points.

When his college days were at an end, Joe had an opportunity to emulate two of his LSU basketball teammates, Frank Brian and Bobby Lowther, and go on into professional basketball, which at that time—the late nineteen-forties—was just growing to maturity. But Adcock, who also had starred in baseball at LSU, chose that sport as a career and signed a contract with the Cincinnati Reds.

Joe spent three seasons, 1950-52, as a part-time performer in the Cincinnati outfield. He played without great distinction, but worked hard, fulfilling a statement made by his basketball coach at LSU, Bernie Moore. Moore called Joe "the greatest competitor I ever coached."

Adcock blossomed into stardom when he was traded to the Braves in the offseason between 1952 and 1953. As a fulltime first baseman with the Braves their first season in Milwaukee, Joe batted a solid .285 and hit eighteen home runs as the Braves made a strong second-place showing.

In 1954, Adcock really hit his home run stride. And now, in the last innings of July 31, he was on the verge of tying or bettering some of the most prestigious batting records in the baseball ledger.

In his first four times at bat against the Dodgers Adcock had unloaded three homers and a double. If he managed a fifth extra base hit in his next time at bat, he would equal a one-game record for the National League that had been set by George Gore of Chicago (two triples, three doubles) in 1885, and matched by Larry Twitchell of Cleveland (one double, three triples, one home run) in 1899. Only one American League player ever had managed five extra base hits in one game—Lou Boudreau of Cleveland, with four doubles and one homer in a 1946 game.

Joe also was close to joining the very select company of men who had belted four home runs in a nine-inning game. Only four players ever had done it—Robert Lowe of Boston in 1894, Ed Delahanty of Philadelphia in 1896, Lou Gehrig of the New York Yankees in 1932, and Gil Hodges of the Brooklyn Dodgers in 1950. Hodges was playing first base for the Dodgers on this day of days for Adcock in 1954.

The game at sweltering Ebbets Field went into the ninth inning. Adcock wasn't the only home run hitter connecting this day. For Brooklyn, Hodges, Don Hoak and Rube Walker all had hit circuit blasts, and Andy Pafko, a former Dodger, and Eddie Mathews, with two homers, had joined Joe in the longball brigade for Milwaukee.

In the bottom of the eighth inning, the Dodgers, who had been trailing badly, 12-2, put across four runs and drove a tiring Burdette out of the game. Burdette was sweating profusely when he was replaced by Bob Buhl, who gave up two hits to the two batters he faced. Dave Jolly, the Braves' relief specialist, finally had to come on to retire the surging Dodgers.

Johnny Podres, a twenty-one-year-old left-hander, was pitching for Brooklyn in the ninth. Before going up to bat Joe Adcock discussed his attempt for a record with Milwaukee coach Johnny Cooney. Cooney had been working with Adcock from the beginning of the season, and had been instrumental in helping Joe improve his hitting. With the Braves comfortably ahead in the score, both Adcock and Cooney agreed that there would be nothing wrong with Joe's swinging for the fences against Podres.

"Usually the last thing you want to do is swing for the home run," Adcock pointed out much later. "That's when you get yourself all fouled up, and you can't do anything right. You're lucky if you even touch the ball."

Cooney advised Joe that, with a left-hander pitching for Brooklyn for the first time, the ball would reach the plate at a different angle than it had when Joe was facing Newcombe, Palica and Wojey, all right-handers. "Just be sure and get under the ball when you swing," Cooney reminded the big first baseman.

There were no runners on base to inspire Adcock to belt one when he stepped in against Podres. Joe didn't need the inspiration. He timed a fastball from Podres perfectly, got under it, as Cooney had advised, and belted it high and far over the left-centerfield fence, his third homer in that vicinity for the afternoon and his fourth for the game. Even the Dodger fans were moved by the magnitude of Adcock's accomplishment. As Joe trotted around the bases with a big grin on his face they stood and gave him thunderous applause.

They still were screaming Joe's name as the Braves remained at bat in the ninth. Milwaukee poured two more runs across and had the bases loaded with two men out and Aaron at the plate. If Hank could get a hit, the next scheduled Braves' batter was Adcock. But Aaron was put out and Joe didn't get a chance to become the only player in major league history to hit *five* homers in a game.

The Dodgers scored one final, meaningless run in the bottom of the ninth to make the final score 15-7 in favor of the Braves. Joe's four homers and a double had resulted in seven RBI's and he had scored five runs himself. "We've got the best hitting room in baseball," Adcock told Mathews with a wide smile. Mathews, Milwaukee's third baseman, was Joe's roommate on road trips. He had slugged two homers of his own.

In the bedlam of the Milwaukee clubhouse it also was disclosed that Adcock's total base collection of eighteen for the afternoon—sixteen on the four homers, and two on the double—were a major league record. No one else ever had compiled more than sixteen total bases in one game. All those with four home runs in one game had managed only those sixteen total bases, and the immortal Ty Cobb of Detroit also had rung up sixteen total bases in one 1925 game, when he hit three homers, a double, and two singles.

The most incredible statistic of all was yet to come. In an analysis of each of Adcock's plate appearances for the day, one fact that hadn't been noticed during the game suddenly became evident. Joe had swung at only five pitches the entire game! In five swings he had registered the most outstanding exhibition of slugging baseball had ever seen.

"Well," Adcock drawled in his Louisiana twang, "it was kinda hot out there. I didn't want to use up all my strength swinging at balls if I wasn't going to hit 'em!"

Saturday, July 31, 1954, at Ebbets Field, Brooklyn

Milwaukee	AB.	R.	H.
Bruton, cf	6	0	4
O'Connell, 2b	5	0	0
Mathews, 3b	4	3	2
Aaron, lf	5	2	2
ADCOCK, 1b	5	5	5
Pafko, rf	4	2	3
Pendleton, rf	1	1	0
Logan, ss	2	1	1
Smalley, ss	2	1	1
Crandall, c	4	0	0
Calderone, c	1	0	1
Wilson, p	1	0	0
Burdette, p	4	0	0
Buhl, p	0	0	0
Jolly, p	0	0	0
Totals	44	15	19

Brooklyn	AB.	R.	H.
Gilliam, 2b	4	1	4
Reese, ss	3	0	1
Zimmer, ss	1	0	0
Snider, cf	4	0	1
Shuba, lf	1	0	0
Hodges, 1b	5	1	1
Amoros, lf-cf	5	2	3
Robinson, 3b	0	0	0
Hoak, 3b	2	1	1
Furillo, rf	5	1	2
Walker, c	5	1	1
Newcombe, p	0	0	0
Labine, p	0	0	0
aMoryn	1	0	0
Palica, p	0	0	0
Wojey, p	1	0	0
bPodres, p	2	0	2
Totals	39	7	16

aHit into double play for Labine in second
bSingled for Wojey in seventh

Milwaukee	1 3 2	0 3 0	3 0 3—15
Brooklyn	1 0 0	0 0 1	0 4 1—7

Error—Hoak. Runs batted in—Mathews 2, Snider, Adcock 7, Logan, Bruton, Hoak 2, Pafko 2, Hodges, Furillo, Walker 2. 2B—Gilliam, Pafko, Bruton 3, Amoros, Adcock, Aaron. 3B—Amoros. HR—Mathews 2, Pafko, Adcock 4, Hoak, Hodges, Walker. Sacrifice fly—Hoak. Double plays—Mathews, O'Connell and Adcock; O'Connell, Logan and Adcock; Zimmer, Gilliam and Hodges. Left on base—Milwaukee 6, Brooklyn 10. Bases on balls off—Burdette 2, Jolly 1, Palica 2. Struck out—by Burdette 3, Jolly 1, Palica 1, Wojey 3, Podres 1. Hits off—Wilson 5 in 1 inning (faced three batters in second), Burdette 8 in 6 1/3, Buhl 2 in 0 (faced two batters in eighth), Jolly 1 in 1 2/3; Newcombe 4 in 1 (faced three batters in second), Labine 1 in 1, Palica 5 in 2 1/3, Wojey 4 in 2 2/3, Podres 5 in 2. Runs and earned runs—off Wilson 1 and 1, Burdette 5 and 5, Jolly 1 and 1; Newcombe 4 and 4, Palica 5 and 5, Wojey 3 and 3, Podres 3 and 2. Wild pitch—Podres. Hit by pitcher—by Wilson (Robinson). Winning pitcher—Burdette (10-11). Losing pitcher—Newcombe (6-6). Umpires—Boggess, Engeln, Stewart and Pinelli. Time—2:53. Attendance—12,263.

Willie's Wondrous Catch

It didn't seem possible that one man could make such a major difference in a ball club, but as the 1954 National League season turned into summer, one man was making the primary difference between a team that had finished a poor fifth in 1953 and a team that was now resting in first place.

The team was the New York Giants, and the man, of course, was Willie Howard Mays, or to most New York fans, simply "Willie."

Willie had arrived in New York in 1951 after tearing up the minor league American Association with his hitting. He was 20 years old, and the Giants, especially manager Leo Durocher, welcomed him gladly. For the young man, playing baseball in the major leagues was a logical extension of his earlier activity.

Willie Mays was born on May 6, 1931, in Westfield, Alabama, a suburb of Birmingham. At 18, he was working in a steel mill. But for Willie baseball always came first. He played in the streets, in the yards, on vacant lots; he played in the morning, he played in the afternoon, and, until summer darkness finally descended, he played at night.

Surprisingly to many, Willie was not an outright sensation in his first year with the Giants, 1951. He batted .274 and clouted 20 home runs, both respectable figures by normal standards, but not quite what had been expected from the young wonder.

Still, Willie made numerous meaningful contributions to the Giants' 1951 pennant drive, the one that finally was capped by Bobby Thomson's memorable home run in the last playoff game against the Brooklyn Dodgers. When Thomson came up for his turn at bat in that fateful ninth inning, Mays was the man in the on-deck circle. Had Thomson not delivered the game-winning blast, Willie might have been the man called upon to decide the 1951 pennant race one way or the other.

Not many weeks had passed in the 1952 baseball season when Willie, like thousands of other 21-year-old men in America, was summoned into military service. He went uncomplainingly though, of course, he would have preferred not to miss the following two seasons of major league competition. Before he exchanged his Giant uniform for khaki, Willie had a meeting with Leo Durocher, the manager.

"Make sure you eat right and stay in good shape, Willie," Durocher told Mays. "When you come back to us, you'll be 23 and I'll expect you to be stronger and bigger. Make sure that you're in great shape to play baseball when you come back to us."

Willie heeded his manager's advice. When he came back to the Giants and joined them at their spring training base in Arizona early in 1954, he was the talk of the exhibition season. His muscles were marvelously honed, his weight evenly distributed over his relatively small but powerful frame. The Dodgers had captured the National league pennant both years that Willie was in the Army, and the Giants had fallen all the way to fifth place in 1953. Clearly, they needed someone who could change their fortunes.

As Mays tore apart exhibition game pitching in the 1954 pre-season contests, Leo Durocher dared to hope that Willie could be the man to reverse the Giants' sagging performance. During the winter he had made a player move that also was to have a significant effect on the Giants' pennant aspirations in 1954. Leo traded Bobby Thomson, the 1951 home run hero, to the Milwaukee Braves, for a pair of relatively unknown left-handed pitchers named Johnny Antonelli and Don Liddle.

Now it was June and two of the new Giants of 1954, Mays and Antonelli, were having superb seasons. Antonelli was pitching victory after victory, and Willie was pounding down the fences all over the National League. He was among the league leaders in every major offensive category and also was playing centerfield as if he had invented the position.

The Giants were in first place, and never were overtaken. The Dodgers, who had run away with the pennant in 1953, didn't challenge in the final weeks of the season, as many had thought they would, and the Giants clinched the flag easily. After a two-year absence from the World Series—the same two years Willie Mays had been absent from the New York lineup —the Giants were back in the fall classic.

Willie completed the regular season with the highest batting average in the league, .345. He also hit 41 home runs, not enough to lead the league but certainly an impressive total. Willie did lead the league in triples with 13 and drove in 110 runs. For these efforts he would later be named the Most Valuable Player of the year in the entire National League.

But all that would be fuel for wintertime conversation and reminiscence. The main task at hand was the World Series, where the Giants faced what seemed an impossible task. Whereas the New Yorkers staged a major surprise by walking off with the National League flag, the American League result was even more surprising.

The New York Yankees, after winning five consecutive pennants and world championships, finally had been beaten. Not just beaten. The Cleveland Indians, managed by Al Lopez, had racked up the finest record of any team in the history of the American League. During the 154-game regular season schedule, the Indians won 111 games and lost only 43.

In winning the National League championship, Durocher's Giants had won 97 against 57 defeats, a solid record but not nearly as impressive as the gaudy mark hung up by the Indians of Al Lopez. Frustrated so often by the Yankees, the Cleveland club was bent on capturing its first World Series title since 1920, and appeared to have all the ingredients to make the job an easy one.

Lopez and his band of Injuns weren't counting on the uncanny success of the Giant pinch hitters, or on a doughty band of underdogs, or on Willie Mays, to upset their victory dance.

The first two games of the World Series were scheduled for the Polo Grounds, which meant the Giants had the advantage of the home field for those two contests. This seemed only small consolation after the Indians' first turn at bat in the first game. The Series began on a Wednesday afternoon, September 29, with two excellent veteran right-handers, Bob Lemon of Cleveland and Sal Maglie of New York, opposing each other on the mound.

Maglie almost failed to get out of the first inning. He hit Al Smith, Cleveland's leftfielder and leadoff batter, with a pitch. Then Bobby Avila, the Indians' second baseman who had led all American League batters during the regular season with a .341 mark, singled.

Maglie retired the next two Indians, but then Vic Wertz, the first baseman, came up. Though he was only 29 years old at the time, Wertz was growing bald prematurely. He looked older than most of the other players in the majors, and his aging appearance was accentuated by the fact that he was not a particularly fast or agile man, either in the field or on the bases.

But Wertz, a muscular left-handed slugger, always could hit the ball hard. This time he picked on a Maglie curveball and knocked it far over the head of Don Mueller, the Giants' rightfielder. By the time Mueller caught up with the ball, both Cleveland baserunners had crossed home plate and Wertz was straddling third base.

Maglie retired the next batter to end the scoring, but the Giants' initial worry about the Cleveland club was confirmed. These Indians were a team to be reckoned with.

New York threatened to score in the bottom of the first inning. With one out, Al Dark, the Giant shortstop, drew a walk and Mueller followed with a single to right. This brought up the Giants' cleanup hitter— Mays. But Lemon, pitching carefully, got Willie to go after the first delivery. Willie hit under the ball and popped it softly to shortstop George Strickland. Then Lemon retired third baseman Hank Thompson and the Indians were out of the inning without a run being scored against them.

After his shaky beginning Maglie regained his control and his composure as he faced the Indians the next couple of innings. He managed to hold Cleveland scoreless while he waited, along with countless Giant fans, for his teammates' bats to explode.

In the third inning, New York scored twice to tie the score. Whitey Lockman singled to open the inning. Then Dark, a master at the hit-and-run maneuver, staged one of his specialties, lining the ball over second base to send Lockman all the way to third base.

There were none out, but the Indians were willing to concede the Giants a run when Lemon got Mueller to bounce into a forceout that cut down Dark at second base. Lockman scored the first run for New York.

This brought up Mays for the second time, and Lemon got himself into further trouble when he walked Willie on four straight pitches out of the strike zone. Hank Thompson, the next batter, promptly lined a sharp single into right to score Mueller and even the score at 2-2.

From that point on, the game settled into a pitching duel between Lemon and Maglie. Both crafty hurlers demonstrated why they had been able to win many games over the years as they mowed down batter after batter through the fourth, fifth, sixth and seventh innings.

About the only Cleveland batter who was able to reach Maglie during those four scoreless innings was Wertz, who had delivered the Indians' two first-inning runs with his mighty triple. In his second and third appearances at the plate against Maglie, Wertz poked singles.

Now it was the top of the eighth, and the 37-year-old Maglie suddenly appeared tired on the mound. A notoriously slow worker, he now was taking even more time than usual between pitches. Larry Doby, the Indians' centerfielder, patiently waited out the Giant pitcher, and eventually drew a walk to lead off the Cleveland eighth. This brought up Al Rosen, Cleveland's slugging third baseman and the fourth man in the batting order.

Rosen was a slow baserunner, and Maglie knew if he could get the Cleveland third baseman to hit the ball to one of the New York infielders, it could be turned into an almost certain double play. But Rosen banged the ball between third and short, and only a miraculous stop by Dark kept the ball from going through into leftfield. All Dark could do was knock the ball down with his bare hand as Rosen crossed first base and Doby went to second.

In the Giant dugout Durocher squirmed fitfully. Here, he knew, would have to come his biggest decision of the afternoon. Should he leave Maglie in to face the next batter, or should he remove his tiring 37-year-old hurler and replace him with a younger, rested relief pitcher?

Durocher reached his decision by considering two things. First of all, the next Indian batter was Wertz, who had gone three-for-three against Maglie already. Secondly, Wertz was a left-handed batter, and the percentages called for a left-handed pitcher to come in to pitch to him.

Durocher made his move. He summoned Don Liddle, the left-hander who had been warming up in the bullpen since the beginning of the inning, and sent Freddie Fitzsimmons, his pitching coach, out to the mound, to tell Maglie his afternoon's labors were done.

Maglie bristled slightly at being removed from the game. He wanted the opportunity to extricate himself from the jam into which he had pitched himself and the rest of the Giants. But as he trudged off the field behind Fitzsimmons, Maglie admitted to himself that he really was tired. If you stay in, he mumbled inwardly, you might really cost us the game. Let someone else take over from here. The Giant fans gave Sal a rousing ovation as he left the field.

Liddle now faced the menacing Wertz, who hadn't made out all afternoon. Perhaps Liddle's left-handed serves would now give the big slugger trouble.

Liddle threw his first pitch, and immediately there was trouble—for the Giants. Wertz met the ball solidly and sent it crashing out toward the deepest portion of right-centerfield. Wertz was to play 17 seasons of major league baseball, and belt 266 lifetime home runs. He may never have hit a ball harder than he did at that precise moment.

The Polo Grounds had one of the deepest center-fields of any stadium in baseball history. The bleachers were an almost unreachable 460 feet away from home plate. As Wertz's blow sailed farther and farther out into centerfield, far over Mays' head, it appeared bound for those bleachers.

Willie, whose instinct for gauging the height and length of a fly ball made him one of the premier defensive outfielders of all time, got a good jump on the ball. His back turned toward the plate, Mays lit out in full flight in pursuit of the ball. He had little chance of catching it, but if he could catch up to it on a bounce fairly quickly, he did have a good chance of preventing at least one Cleveland run. Doby, who was on second base, certainly would score. But perhaps the slow-footed Rosen could be held at third and Wertz could be held at second.

Finally Willie was a few feet in front of the bleacher wall. He had his arms stretched out in front of him, his glove up.

And the ball fell into his glove with Mays still on a dead run.

The ball had barely disappeared into the safety of Mays' glove when Willie spun around backward and unfurled a mighty throw, losing his cap in the effort. The throw reached Davey Williams, the Giant second baseman, in back of the base on one bounce, and prevented Doby from advancing more than one base. Rosen had to scramble to get safely back to first. Both Cleveland runners were left on base as the next two Indians were retired easily.

Mays' incredible catch had saved the game for the Giants. Expert observers at the game, former players and sportswriters alike, insisted it was the greatest catch ever made, certainly the greatest in a World Series game. In later years, when Willie would be asked to name the most important catch he ever had made, he would reply, "No contest. The catch I made on Wertz in the opening game of the 1954 World Series."

Joe DiMaggio, who witnessed the catch in person, marveled at the play. What was truly remarkable about the catch, DiMaggio pointed out, was Mays' judgment in not allowing the fence to scare him away from making the catch nearly 460 feet away from the plate.

While he never minimized the importance of his great eighth-inning catch, Willie felt that another fine defensive play he made in the same game was overlooked.

"I got a lot of publicity out of my catch off Wertz," he said in later years. "Some writers claimed it was the greatest defensive play they ever saw in a World Series. The truth is, I made a greater defensive play two innings later, and hardly anybody noticed it."

Willie referred to the tenth-inning play he made on another ball hit by Wertz, who enjoyed an overall super-slugging day. Mays didn't catch this one. No one could have. The score still was tied at 2-2 as the game went into extra innings. Marv Grissom, the ace of the Giants' bullpen, was working on the mound for New York by this time. Grissom's best pitch was a screwball, which broke away from left-handed batters.

One of Grissom's screwballs didn't break far enough away from Wertz, who socked a long foul to leftfield, his opposite field.

"That long foul should have convinced me to play Wertz more over to leftfield," Mays recalls. "But for some reason or other I wasn't thinking and continued to play him in right-center. Maybe I was still thinking of that ball he'd hit in the eighth inning.

"Sure enough, Wertz hit the next ball to left-center. It was the toughest chance I had in the entire Series.

The ball was mean when it landed and it hopped, and I had to play it at an angle. I just managed to grab it one-handed and held Wertz to a double. Had it gone through, it would have been an inside-the-park home run."

As it turned out, Wertz never advanced farther than third base. Grissom finally got the Indians out in the top of the tenth. In the bottom of the inning Dusty Rhodes, a pinch-hitting sensation for the Giants all season, came off the bench and whacked a three-run pinch-hit homer off Lemon into the rightfield stands to give New York a 5-2 victory.

The Giants went on to an incredible four-game sweep over the highly favored Indians. But they probably never would have won even one game if it weren't for the fielding heroics of their wondrous centerfielder, Willie Mays.

Wednesday, September 29, 1954, at Polo Grounds, New York

Cleveland (A)	AB.	R.	H.	New York (N)	AB.	R.	H.
Smith, lf	4	1	1	Lockman, 1b	5	1	1
Avila, 2b	5	1	1	Dark, ss	4	0	2
Doby, cf	3	0	1	Mueller, rf	5	1	2
Rosen, 3b	5	0	1	MAYS, cf	3	1	0
Wertz, 1b	5	0	4	Thompson, 3b	3	1	1
dRegalado	0	0	0	Irvin, lf	3	0	0
Grasso, c	0	0	0	fRhodes	1	1	1
Philley, rf	3	0	0	Williams, 2b	4	0	0
aMajeski	0	0	0	Westrum, c	4	0	2
bMitchell	0	0	0	Maglie, p	3	0	0
Dente, ss	0	0	0	Liddle, p	0	0	0
Strickland, ss	3	0	0	Grissom, p	1	0	0
cPope, rf	1	0	0				
Hegan, c	4	0	0	Totals	36	5	9
eGlynn, 1b	1	0	0				
Lemon, p	4	0	0				
Totals	38	2	8g				

aAnnounced as batter for Philley in eighth
bWalked for Majeski in eighth
cCalled out on strikes for Strickland in eighth
dRan for Wertz in tenth
eStruck out for Hegan in tenth
fHit home run for Irvin in tenth
gOne out when winning run scored

Cleveland	2 0 0	0 0 0	0 0 0	0—2
New York	0 0 2	0 0 0	0 0 0	3—5

Runs batted in—Wertz 2, Mueller, Thompson, Rhodes 3. Two-base hit—Wertz. Three-base hit—Wertz. Home run—Rhodes. Stolen base—Mays. Sacrifice hits—Irvin, Dente. Left on bases—Cleveland 13, New York 9. Earned runs—New York 5, Cleveland 2. Bases on balls—Lemon 5, Maglie 2, Grissom 3. Strikeouts—Maglie 2, Grissom 2, Lemon 6. Hits off—Maglie 7 in 7 innings (pitched to two batters in eighth); Liddle 0 in 1/3; Grissom 1 in 2 2/3. Hit by pitcher—by Maglie (Smith). Wild pitch—Lemon. Winning pitcher—Grissom. Losing pitcher—Lemon. Umpires—Barlick, Berry, Conlan, Stevens, Warneke, Napp. Time—3:11. Attendance—52,751.

World Series Perfection

Before he took the mound for the New York Yankees on the brilliant Monday afternoon of October 8, 1956, it would have been difficult to find a more unlikely candidate for the Hall of Fame than Donald James Larsen.

Up to that time, the 27-year-old right-handed pitcher had compiled a record, both on and off the field, that seemed to lead nowhere but to oblivion. Not that he wasn't endowed with considerable physical equipment. On the contrary, perhaps he was blessed with an overabundance of natural ability. He stood 6-4 and weighed 230 pounds and could fire a baseball as hard as anybody in the major leagues when he wanted to.

But he didn't always seem to want to. Though stardom had been predicted for him from the moment he reported to the training camp of the St. Louis Browns in 1953, Larsen had fallen far short of expectations. He posted a 7-12 record with the 1953 Browns. The team left St. Louis the following season and became the Baltimore Orioles. Larsen became the losingest pitcher in the big leagues, tumbling to a 3-21 record, a horrendous mark.

But the Yankees, who had seen their streak of five consecutive American League championships snapped by the Cleveland Indians in 1954, thought they saw something in the strong-armed, powerfully built Larsen. So they acquired him in a trade. They reasoned that, with a stronger club than the Orioles supporting him, Larsen could be a big winner.

It hadn't worked out that way. Though the Yankees climbed back on top of the American League standings in 1955, Larsen was only a minor contributor to the championship effort. He won nine games and lost two. Casey Stengel, the New York manager, gave the big right-hander a start in the World Series against the Brooklyn Dodgers, and Larsen was belted out of the box after four innings. He had given up five runs and was charged with a defeat. The Dodgers eventually captured the Series from the Yankees, four games to three.

In 1956, Larsen pitched almost as much in relief as he did as a starter. Of his 38 mound appearances, 20 were starts and 18 were relief stints. His won-lost record was impressive on the surface—eleven victories, five defeats—but it wasn't difficult to post a winning record for the domineering Yankees, who again captured the American League flag.

The Dodgers provided the opposition in the 1956 World Series, as they had in 1955. Intent on successfully defending their world championship, the Dodgers got off to a quick start in the first game at Ebbets Field, their home park. Sal Maglie, the 39-year-old curveball specialist who had been considered washed up by the Giants, with whom he spent the major part of his career, outpitched Yankee left-hander Whitey Ford as Brooklyn won the opener, 6-3.

Stengel surprised many observers when he sent Larsen to the mound to start the second game for New York. He seemed to be overmatched against Brooklyn's Don Newcombe, who had won 27 games during the regular season.

But the Yankees attacked Newcombe for six runs inside of two innings, driving him from the mound with a five-run outburst in the second capped by a grand slam home run off the bat of catcher Yogi Berra.

Larsen himself delivered the fifth run in the Yankee second, hitting a single that scored second baseman Billy Martin. It all added up to a 6-0 lead for Larsen and the Yankees, as the Dodgers came up in the bottom of the second. Normally a six-run lead in the second inning is a pitcher's dream. But for Larsen it quickly became a nightmare.

Before they had completed their turn at bat, the Dodgers had tied the score with six runs. An error by Joe Collins at first base hurt Larsen's efforts, but he hurt himself more by walking four batters before he was yanked from the game by Stengel with one run in and the bases loaded. The relief pitching was awful for the Yankees. After Brooklyn tied the score that inning, the Dodgers cuffed up six other Yankee hurlers for a 13-8 victory and a commanding two-game lead in the Series.

In the friendlier confines of Yankee Stadium, the Bronx Bombers moved back into contention for the world title by stopping the Dodgers in the third game, 5-3, and again in the fourth game, 6-2, Whitey Ford, pitching with only two days rest, hurled a masterful eight-hitter to win the third game. Tom Sturdivant, a 16-game winner for the Yanks in the regular season, was the fourth-game winner.

The fifth game, also scheduled for Yankee Stadium, loomed as the most crucial of the postseason competition. Brooklyn manager Walter Alston nominated Maglie, the winner of the first game, as his starter in this all-important contest. There was some question on the part of observers and newsmen over the identity of the Yankee pitcher for this game. Most thought that right-hander Johnny Kucks deserved the starting nod. In New York's drive to the pennant, Kucks had won 18 games, second best on the team only to Ford's 19 victories.

But Stengel crossed up the experts. He chose Larsen as his starter. As soon as Stengel announced his choice, the critics mounted an attack. Hadn't Stengel's strategy backfired in the second game when he started Larsen? Hadn't Larsen been consistently inconsistent all year, hardly deserving the opportunity for another Series start?

Stengel stuck to his choice. Fans and reporters could be fickle, he knew. After he had taken Larsen out of the second game, the Yankee manager had been criticized for his quick hook. To that criticism, Stengel had retorted. "It might get him on his toes for his next start!" He never imagined Larsen could be that much on his toes only three days later.

Both Larsen and Stengel elected to write off Don's failure in the second game of the Series as an accident. Actually, toward the end of the '56 season, Larsen had been reasonably effective. Late in the year, Don had decided to eliminate his extensive windup before delivering the pitch. He thought that opposing coaches might be stealing his pitches, and he was resolved to do something about it. With the persmission of pitching coach Jim Turner, Don went to a no-windup style of pitching. He found it had advantages that went beyond making his pitches less susceptible to being "read" by rival coaches.

"It gave me better control to pitch without a windup," Don recalled later. "I took nothing off my fastball and kept the batters tense."

So Larsen took his no-windup style to the mound for the Yankees against the Dodgers' Maglie for the fifth game of the 1956 World Series.

Long before he had arrived at this crucial stage of his major league baseball career, Don Larsen seemed to be on the road to athletic stardom. Born in Michigan City, Indiana, in 1929, he was taken by his family to

San Diego, California, when he was very young, and grew up in that southern California city. He grew into a big, strong teenager, and by the time he reached high school Don was known as a formidable baseball and basketball player in the area. At Point Loma High School, young Larsen excelled more at basketball than baseball, though he preferred the latter.

Though he was a reasonably successful pitcher, it was the hitting part of baseball that really appealed to Don. "I always could hit pretty well," he reminisced in later years. "It came kind of natural to me. Pitching was different. I really had to work hard at that."

Because of his hitting prowess, many teams considered using Larsen as an outfielder or first baseman. He actually got into two major league games as an outfielder, and often was used as a pinch hitter during his fourteen-year career in the majors. When he finally left the big leagues, Don had compiled a lifetime batting average of .242, far better than most pitchers in history, and had walloped 14 home runs.

Don's hitting notwithstanding, his powerful arm and his physical dimensions attracted scouts to Larsen's games in the late 1940s. When he graduated from Point Loma, Don received several offers to attend college on basketball scholarships. But he hardly considered those offers for a moment. Baseball was his love, and he accepted a $150-a-month contract to pitch for a farm team of the St. Louis Browns. It was a rather lowly farm team—Aberdeen, South Dakota, in the Class C Northern League. But Larsen went without complaint.

Finally reaching the Browns in 1953, Don promptly put his name into the pitching record book—as a hitter. Over a period of three games, he delivered seven straight hits, an all-time mark for pitchers.

The rest of his rookie season with the Browns was rather undistinguished—on the mound, that is. Away from the ball park, Don began carving out a reputation around St. Louis that was less than honorable. He quickly earned the nickname "Nightrider" because of his affinity for the night life in the Gaslight City.

In 1954, Larsen found Baltimore even more to his liking than St. Louis, and had several clashes with manager Jimmy Dykes over the pitcher's failure to heed the curfew time.

Casey Stengel must have known about Larsen's off-the-field shenanigans when Don came to the Yankees in 1955. But old Casey, who could raise a drink with anybody who ever lived in baseball, was given to winking at a ballplayer's night life—as long as the player performed on the field.

Stengel was not so lenient that he allowed players to report out of shape. Perhaps auditioning for the glittering social whirl of New York, Don spent much of the offseason between the 1954 and 1955 campaigns falling out of top physical condition. When he reported to the Yankees' camp in Florida, he was badly overweight and also was nursing a sore right shoulder.

Larsen still hadn't rounded into the form the Yankees expected of him by the opening of the season. By early May, he had won just one game—and a nickname that alluded to his erratic behavior: "Gooneybird." Stengel saw no alternative but to ship Don back to the minors. Larsen was sent to the Yankees' farm team in Denver.

Don, of course, was not at all happy about going. "I don't care if I ever come back!" he griped to his teammates as he packed to move west. "Take it easy, Don," Mickey Mantle advised him. "Listen, they sent me out a few years ago, too. But as soon as I started going good, they called me right back. They'll do it for you too, as soon as you show you can pitch." Late in July Larsen was a Yankee again.

He still was not the prototype Boy Scout, but Don

had learned to tone down his activities away from the diamond. Now, more than a year later, with a skeptical capacity crowd looking on in cavernous Yankee Stadium, Larsen faced the most important moment of his career. Another performance like the one he had given in Ebbets Field three days earlier and Don might have written his farewell as a Yankee.

The night before the fifth game, Larsen was driving home with Art Richman, a baseball writer for the New York *Daily Mirror,* who was a good friend of Don's. They started talking about the upcoming fifth game, and Larsen, perhaps to keep his mind off the importance his pitching efforts would play in the critical contest, talked about hitting, the talent that always had come more naturally to him.

"Wouldn't it be funny," he asked Richman, "if I hit a grand slam off Maglie and we won the game?"

Don didn't get any hits at all off Maglie, as it turned out. For a time it must have seemed to the huge crowd of 64,519 fans that no one on either team was capable of getting a hit off either Maglie or Larsen.

In the first three innings, every Dodger and every Yankee who came to bat was retired. Maglie's curveballs and sinkerballs were crackling across the plate to perfection. Larsen, delivering his pitches without benefit of windup, was cleverly mixing up his fastballs with sliders.

The only thing that came close to a hit in the first three innings was a ball hit by Jackie Robinson, leading off the Dodger second. The Brooklyn third baseman lashed the ball directly at his counterpart, Yankee third baseman Andy Carey. The ball was hit so hard that it deflected off Carey's glove toward Gil McDougald, the shortstop. McDougald quickly grabbed the bouncing ball and rifled it across the diamond to first baseman Joe Collins. Robinson, straining all the way, nearly beat the ball to the base. But he was out by half a step.

Robinson was 37 years old when he played in the 1956 World Series. Graying and slightly overweight, Jackie was no longer the ballplayer he had been in his early years with the Dodgers. No one realized it at the time, but the 1956 Series represented Jackie's farewell to baseball. He retired from the game before the 1957 season to close out a brilliant ten-year career. Most observers at the fifth game of the '56 Series felt that the Jackie Robinson of a few years earlier would have beaten out his second-inning infield drive.

In the fourth inning, Larsen again set the Dodgers down in order. Duke Snider, the slugging centerfielder, nearly broke the spell when he lined a long shot into the lower deck in rightfield. But it was clearly foul. Snider then took a called third strike for the third out.

The Yankees came up for their second lineup go-round in the bottom of the fourth. Maglie kept mowing down batters as he retired Hank Bauer and Collins with ease, and got two strikes on Mantle. On the next pitch Mickey poked a drive down the rightfield line that landed in the lower stands—just inside the foul pole for a home run. Mantle, the twenty-fourth batter in the game, had been the first to reach base safely, and his hit allowed him to circle the bases.

Berra followed Mantle's homer with a long drive to centerfield. Snider raced far to his right to make a spectacular diving catch at his shoestrings. But the Yankees now had one big run, and the way this game was going, even a one-run edge loomed large.

The Dodgers were determined to erase the Yanks' edge as they batted in the top of the fifth inning. This proved to be Larsen's toughest inning of the day—the Dodgers almost got two hits.

With one out, Gil Hodges, Brooklyn's slugging first

baseman, drove the ball into deep left centerfield, where Mantle, running at top speed, made a backhand catch.

The next batter was leftfielder Sandy Amoros, whose startling catch to start a double play in the seventh game of the 1955 World Series turned out to be the decisive play in the Dodgers' Series win. Amoros jumped on Larsen's one-one pitch and sent it into the rightfield seats. It landed almost exactly where Mantle's home run had landed just moments before. But umpire Ed Runge, who had closely followed the flight of the ball from the moment it left the bat, ruled it had fallen foul by a few inches. Given this reprieve, Larsen got Amoros to ground out to second baseman Billy Martin to end the inning.

When Larsen again retired the Dodgers in order in the sixth inning, he suddenly noticed that his teammates were acting strangely when he returned to the Yankee dugout. They seemed to be deliberately avoiding him, looking in another direction when he approached, talking to someone else when he attempted conversation. Don shot a quick glance at manager Stengel, but Casey was busy talking to Mantle.

Squinting his eyes to escape the glare of the bright October sun, Larsen looked out into right centerfield and found the answer to why his teammates were acting so strangely. The scoreboard showed the Dodger totals for six innings as three big, round zeros—no runs, no hits, no errors. Not until then did Don realize he was working on a no-hitter, let alone a perfect game.

"Then I thought about it for a minute and realized that I hadn't given up any hits," Larsen later recalled. "But the perfect game thing didn't register at all until later. I thought I had given up a walk or two somewhere along the line."

In the history of the World Series, which began in

1903, no pitcher ever had thrown a no-hit game. Now Don was only nine outs away. But he couldn't afford the luxury of thinking about it a great deal. With only a one-run lead, his main mission was to protect that advantage. If the no-hitter were to come, it would come. Fate would have to make that decision.

The Yankee batters realized that their pitcher was under severe pressure with only the slim lead. In the sixth, they got to Maglie for another run. They almost broke the game wide open. Carey opened the inning by bouncing a single over Maglie's head. Larsen, aiding his own cause, sacrificed Carey to second with a pressure bunt on two strikes. Had the bunt gone foul, Don would have been a strikeout victim.

Bauer hammered a single between third and short, driving home Carey from second base. Then Collins singled to right, sending Bauer to third. With Mantle due at the plate, the Yankees had only one out and Maglie faced his most dangerous situation of the afternoon. If Mickey hit safely, it seemed almost certain that Maglie would be removed from the mound.

Mantle hit the ball sharply, but right at Hodges, who stepped on first to retire Mickey. The alert first baseman then threw home to Campanella, as Bauer, who had broken home with the pitch to Mantle, was trapped off third base. Campanella and Robinson ran him down, and Robinson finally tagged Bauer out to complete a double play.

Now Larsen was the center of attention as the game moved into its final three innings. The frustrated Dodgers were hoping desperately to get at least one man on base and have a chance to get back into the ballgame. But in the top of the seventh, Jim Gilliam, Pee Wee Reese and Snider came up to face Larsen, and each of the three was denied.

As Larsen came out for the top of the eighth, the

fans seated in Yankee Stadium were in a frenzy. They yelled encouragement to Don as he toed the mound, then fell silent as he reached back to throw. As each batter was retired, they held their breath ever tighter. Robinson was the first out in the eighth. Then Hodges, who had chased Mantle deep into left centerfield for his fifth-inning drive, connected solidly again. This time he hit a low liner to third. Carey, moving quickly and adroitly to his left, stabbed the ball with his glove before it reached the ground.

Amoros ended the Brooklyn half of the eighth by flying to Mantle, and Larsen now had retired twenty-four consecutive batters.

Shadows were beginning to fall in the Yankee Stadium outfield as late afternoon approached. By now everyone in the stands, Dodger fans included, was caught up in the drama that was unfolding. Larsen was only three outs away from accomplishing the impossible—a perfect game in the World Series! No one had pitched a perfect game in the major leagues since 1922, when a White Sox pitcher named Charley Robertson accomplished the feat. That was a regular-season masterpiece. Now here was Larsen on the verge of perfection in baseball's most important annual competition.

Yankee fans, praying that the miracle would continue, sat impatiently as the home team took its turn at bat in the bottom of the eighth. No one wanted to see the Yankees bat. The hitters were not the story; Larsen was. The odds on a Yankee Stadium crowd cheering three straight New York strikeouts are enormous. But that's just what this Yankee Stadium crowd did. Maglie fanned Larsen, Bauer and Collins in order. Yankee fans never cheered louder for a home run hit by any of their heroes down through the years.

The stage was set for history. Larsen came to the mound for the ninth inning. The Yankee infielders, who had maintained a constant chatter all afternoon, were nearly silent. Only scrappy Billy Martin at second base was moved to speak.

"Come on, Don," Martin shouted. "Fire that ball!"

Don was too preoccupied to hear Martin, or to turn around to face him. His eyes were riveted on the mitt on catcher Berra's hand, and the man at the plate, the Dodger rightfielder, Carl Furillo. One of the most popular Brooklyn players, Furillo was a dangerous clutch hitter, a former National League batting champion.

Furillo was prepared to wait Larsen out if he could. He fouled off Don's first two pitches, took a ball, then fouled off two more into the stands in short rightfield. Obviously, Furillo was attempting to slice the ball into rightfield for a base hit.

Don peered in for the sign from Berra, tugged at his belt and threw a fastball. Sure enough, Furillo hit the ball out to rightfield. But Bauer was right there and hauled it in for the out.

Campanella was next up. The portly Dodger catcher had suffered a poor season in 1956, but always was a formidable threat to drive the ball out of sight. Larsen could hardly afford to relax against Campy. Berra walked slowly out to the mound. "They're still in the game," he reminded Don. "That's the main thing you've got to worry about." Yogi was right. The Yankee lead of 2-0 could not be considered insurmountable. A hit here, followed by a homer by any of several Brooklyn belters, and it would be a brand-new ballgame.

Larsen worked carefully to Campanella. The Brooklyn receiver swung at the first pitch, a fastball, and fouled it down the leftfield line. Don tried a curveball next. Campanella offered at it and hit an easy ground ball to Martin at second base, who threw him out.

The fans roared. Now there was only one more out to go. The tension was unbearable. The fans in the stands sat in deathly silence, not daring to utter a sound lest the spell of the moment be shattered. All over New York City people paused by their television sets or radios and stopped whatever they were doing. Executives in pinstripes and carrying attaché cases stopped transistor-carrying messenger boys in the streets, demanding, "What's happening now? How many more outs to go?"

Up in the radio broadcast booth, Bob Wolff wet his lips with his tongue. A veteran broadcaster of wide experience, Wolff felt the tenseness and drama of the occasion as much as anybody. But while most people who watched and listened did so in breathless silence, Wolff had to continue talking.

Maglie was the scheduled batter for the Dodgers. He had pitched valiantly, allowing the potent Yankee lineup only two runs and five hits in eight innings. But Dodger manager Alston replaced him with pinch hitter Dale Mitchell. A left-handed batter, Mitchell was a professional with a bat in his hands. He had enjoyed several outstanding seasons with the Cleveland Indians and was a lifetime .312 hitter. One season, 1948, he had hit as high as .336. Now thirty-five years old, Mitchell had been acquired from the Indians in the middle of the 1956 campaign. He had gotten into nineteen games for Brooklyn as a pinch hitter, and delivered several timely hits, batting .292.

A tough man to strike out and not a threat to hit a longball, Mitchell's mission was obvious. He had been sent up by Alston to look over Larsen's pitches, pick out a good one, and hit a single. Singles were Mitchell's specialty. He had a faculty for looping, popping, dribbling and lashing hits just out of the reach of fielders. He was just the kind of batter that has ruined many a no-hit effort.

Larsen was well aware of Mitchell's knack. He had

faced him many times when Mitchell was playing with Cleveland. After consulting with Berra, Don decided that there was no room for finesse now. His first pitch to Mitchell was a fastball. It went wide and plate umpire Babe Pinelli yelled, "Ball!"

Berra realized that Larsen was carrying an almost unbelievable burden of pressure on his back. The Yankee catcher felt that he had to keep Don from taking too much time thinking about what he was going to do next. This was a time for throwing, not thinking. Yogi returned the ball swiftly to Larsen and signaled another fastball. He would keep signaling fastballs the rest of the way. Larsen's fastball still was humming as if it were the first inning, and the shadows that were descending faster and faster over the stadium made it difficult for the batter to follow the ball well.

Don's second fastball to Mitchell buzzed across the plate. Mitchell didn't offer at it, but it clearly was a strike, and Pinelli raised his right hand to confirm it.

Larsen got the ball back quickly again from Berra, and almost as quickly he threw again toward the plate. Mitchell swung violently at the flying ball—and missed. Strike two.

One more strike. Everyone in the stands was on the verge of exhaustion. Not a soul dared to draw breath, and the sound of more than 64,000 mouths sucking in small gasps of air was about the only sound in the tiers of the mammoth stadium.

Mitchell stood in at the plate again, erect in the left-handed batter's box. Larsen threw again, seeking the final strike. Mitchell got only a piece of it and fouled it off to the left into the crowd. The agony was prolonged still further when Mitchell stepped out of the batter's box and stooped down for a handful of dirt. He rubbed the dirt into his perspiring palms for what seemed like hours. Actually, Mitchell took only a few seconds performing one of baseball's most time-honored rituals. Ninety-nine per cent of the time, no one would have thought anything of it.

But this time was different, very different. Finally Mitchell stepped in again. The count still was one ball, two strikes. Larsen peered at Berra's mitt, then at the batter. For a split second, total silence covered the entire ballpark. The ball came hurtling at Mitchell.

Larsen's ninety-seventh pitch of the day was a good one. It headed for an outside corner of the plate. It was the kind of pitch Mitchell had swung at on many other occasions and poked into leftfield. He cocked his bat as if ready to do just that. Then he held up, thinking the ball would miss the corner.

Mitchell was wrong.

"Strike three!" bellowed umpire Pinelli.

Don Larsen had done it—twenty-seven men up, twenty-seven men down! As Yankee Stadium erupted in bedlam, Berra jumped into Larsen's arms at the mound, creating a great picture for the legions of photographers who swarmed around the pitcher. There was stubby Yogi Berra, just five feet, eight inches tall, climbing into the arms of the six-foot, four-inch pitcher, the man who had just turned in the most remarkable job of pitching in World Series history.

Larsen's perfect game spurred the Yanks on to the world championship, which they captured two days later with another shutout victory, 9-0.

Pinelli, who had umpired behind the plate during Larsen's masterpiece, worked at second base the day the Bombers clinched the World Series title. In the umpires' dressing room after the seventh game, he announced his retirement after a long, distinguished career as one of the men in blue.

"I was thinking I might retire after this year's Series," Pinelli told reporters. "Now I'm certain. How can I ever umpire another game behind the plate after umpiring a perfect game in the World Series? It could never be the same again. Now I've seen it all."

Here is the play-by-play of Don Larsen's perfect game against the Brooklyn Dodgers in the fifth game of the 1956 World Series, the manner in which he retired 27 consecutive batters:

FIRST INNING

Gilliam: Ball 1, foul down first-base line, ball 2, strike 2 called, strike 3 called. Reese: Strike 1 foul, ball 1, strike 2 called, ball 2, ball 3, strike 3 called. Snider: Ball 1, strike 1, ball 2, lined to Bauer in right.

SECOND INNING

Robinson: Strike 1 called, hit liner which caromed off glove of third baseman Carey to shortstop McDougald, who threw him out by less than a step. Hodges: Ball 1, strike 1, strike 2 called, fanned on low outside curve. Amoros: Strike 1, strike 2 foul, ball 1, ball 2, popped to second baseman Martin, who back-pedaled and held on to ball as he toppled over.

THIRD INNING

Furillo: Strike 1 called, flied to Bauer. Campanella: Ball 1, strike 1 called, strike 2, strike 3 swinging. Maglie: Lined to Mantle in center on first pitch.

FOURTH INNING

Gilliam: Grounded out, Martin to Collins, on first pitch. Reese: Tried to check swing at first pitch, but tapped to Martin. Snider: Ball 1, ball 2 low, strike 1, long foul into lower deck, strike 2 called, foul to left as count holds, took a called third strike down the middle.

FIFTH INNING

Robinson: Ball 1, strike 1 foul, strike 2 on change-up, long foul to left, flied fairly deep to Bauer. Hodges: Strike 1 called, strike 2 called, ball 1, ball 2, sent Mantle deep into left-center for one-handed catch. Amoros: Ball 1, strike 1 called, lined ball foul down rightfield line into lower deck, ball 2, rolled out, Martin to Collins.

SIXTH INNING

Furillo: Strike 1 foul, popped to Martin in short right. Campanella: Popped to Martin in short center on first pitch. Maglie: Strike 1, strike 2, ball 1, foul, foul, ball 2, struck out.

SEVENTH INNING

Gilliam: Strike 1 called, ball 1, strike 2 foul to left, hit sharply to McDougald, who took ball on short hop and threw to Collins at first for the out. Reese: Strike 1 foul back on screen, flied deep to Mantle. Snider: Ball 1, flied to Slaughter in left.

EIGHTH INNING

Robinson: Strike 1 called, strike 2 foul, bounced out, Larsen to Collins. Hodges: Strike 1 called, ball 1 high, strike 2 swinging, ball 2 outside, hit low liner on which Carey, moving to his left, made a one-handed stab. Amoros: Strike 1 called, flied deep to Mantle, who had to move to his left.

NINTH INNING

Furillo: Strike 1 foul, strike 2 foul, ball 1 high, foul into first base box seats, another foul into the right-field boxes, flied to Bauer. Campanella: Strike 1 foul, grounded out, Martin to Collins. Mitchell, batting for

Maglie: Ball 1 outside, strike 1 called, strike 2 swinging, foul to the left into the crowd, strike 3 called.

Monday, October 8, 1956, at Yankee Stadium

Brooklyn (N)	AB.	R.	H.
Gilliam, 2b	3	0	0
Reese, ss	3	0	0
Snider, cf	3	0	0
Robinson, 3b	3	0	0
Hodges, 1b	3	0	0
Amoros, lf	3	0	0
Furillo, rf	3	0	0
Campanella, c	3	0	0
Maglie, p	2	0	0
aMitchell	1	0	0
Totals	27	0	0

New York (A)	AB.	R.	H.
Bauer, rf	4	0	1
Collins, 1b	4	0	1
Mantle, cf	3	1	1
Berra, c	3	0	0
Slaughter, lf	2	0	0
Martin, 2b	3	0	1
McDougald, ss	2	0	0
Carey, 3b	3	1	1
LARSEN, p	2	0	0
Totals	26	2	5

aCalled out on strikes for Maglie in ninth

```
Brooklyn .............. 0 0 0   0 0 0   0 0 0—0
New York .............. 0 0 0   1 0 1   0 0 x—2
```

Errors—None. Runs batted in—Mantle, Bauer. Home run—Mantle. Sacrifice hit—Larsen. Double plays—Reese and Hodges; Hodges, Campanella, Robinson; Campanella and Robinson. Left on base—Dodgers 0, Yankees 3. Bases on balls—Maglie 2. Strikeouts—Larsen 7, Maglie 5. Winner—Larsen. Loser—Maglie. Umpires—Pinelli, Soar, Boggess, Napp, Gorman, Runge. Time—2:06. Attendance—64,519.

Ted Williams' Last Game

Following his remarkable .388 batting average for the 1957 season at the age of 39, Ted Williams signed a two-year contract with the Boston Red Sox. Everyone, Ted included, imagined it would be his last contract to play baseball in the major leagues, where he had been belting baseballs for the Boston Red Sox since 1939.

Despite missing three full seasons, 1943-45, and most of two others, 1952 and 1953, in military service, Williams had compiled feats of batting and slugging that ranked him at the forefront of all those who had put bat to baseball in all the years of major league baseball. As a hitter for average, The Splendid Splinter, so named because of his marvelously trim frame—six feet three inches, 190 pounds at the peak of his career— was among the top five batsmen on record; as a prodigious slugger, he ranked behind only Babe Ruth in all-time extra base hitting, leading the American League nine times in slugging percentage and reaching base at a faster rate per at-bats than anyone else, including the fabulous Babe.

Ted was a center of controversy as well as excitement in Boston during most of his playing career, because of his often intemperate relationship with the press and the fans. He resolved to close his career on a high note during his final two years. In 1958, he accomplished something no one else ever had done: he won the American League batting championship at the age of forty. Williams overtook a teammate, first baseman Pete Runnels, in the closing days of the campaign, and captured the crown with a .328 mark to .322 for a disappointed Runnels. It was the sixth batting title for Ted, and by all odds the most remarkable, coming as it did at his advanced age. It was more remarkable even than his first bat title, achieved with a .406 average in 1941 when he was twenty-three. Three decades later, the only one to come close to Williams' .400-plus average of 1941 was Ted himself, with his .388 in 1957. That year he batted an incredible .453 for the second half of the schedule, and finished the season only five hits short of another .400 batting average.

Still, Ted felt if he could maintain a reasonable pace for 1959, he could close his career on a high note. Relaxing during the offseason in his favorite way—fishing in the deep seas off the Florida coast—Williams hurt his neck and was in traction much of the time in 1959. Ted also was in misery because he was able to contribute only ten home runs and forty-three runs batted in for one hundred and three games, many of those limited to just one time at bat as a pinch hitter. More appalling still was Ted's tumble to a .254 average, by far the lowest of his tremendous career. His previous low over a full season was his rookie campaign of 1939 when he clouted a robust .327.

A .254 average wasn't quite the way Williams had intended to go out. Convinced that his nagging neck injury had been the source of most of his troubles in 1959, he prevailed upon Tom Yawkey, owner of the Red Sox, to let him try another season. Ted was hurt when Yawkey gently suggested he might be better off if he called it a career right then.

"I was burned up," Williams later recalled. "I mean, after all, I had been around a few years and had showed I could play a little. I wanted at least to wait until the next year's spring training to see if I still could do anything. I didn't want to end on a bad year, and if I saw in 1960 that I really wasn't going to be able to play, I would have been the first to tell Tom. To show Tom I meant what I said, I volunteered to have my salary reduced to $90,000 from $125,000, almost a twenty-five per cent reduction. The deal was that if I came back and did well, he would pay me at my old salary."

Whatever Ted finally received by way of salary from Yawkey in 1960, he was worth every nickel. Williams completely vindicated himself for his lacklustre performance of 1959. Ahead of his time with open-necked sport shirts and eschewer of ties, Ted didn't look old-fashioned at the plate in 1960, the fourth calendar decade in which he had appeared in the big leagues.

Ted himself and many others had despaired of his reaching the 500-homer plateau, a mark he would have reached with ease had he not spent so much time in military service. Entering the 1960 campaign, Williams still was eight circuit blasts short of half a thousand. Though he batted just three hundred and ten times officially, Ted passed five hundred homers with ease in the spring.

The Red Sox were a shoddy outfit in 1960. But for the presence of the even shoddier Kansas City Athletics in the same eight-team American League, the Boston club would have fallen out of the bottom of the league. The Red Sox, despite Williams' numerous heroics, were a poor seventh place club. Ted was about the only gate attraction, and little wonder. Despite his athletic old age, he still was the best the club had to offer. It had been that way for a very long time.

Theodore Samuel Williams was born on August 30, 1918, in San Diego, California, and from the beginning, sports filled his life. "I was lucky to grow up in southern California," he said many years later. "I never was much good at anything but sports, and in southern California the weather was always warm and you could play ball as late as you wanted almost all year round. But I played everything then—horseshoes, handball, *everything!*"

Ted's parents had difficulty making ends meet during the years of the depression that ravaged the United States in the nineteen-thirties. His father had a small photographic shop, and his mother worked for the Salvation Army. Both worked very long hours and Ted, an only child, would have been alone a great deal of the time but for the hours he spent competing in sports and games with other boys in San Diego. Always tall and extremely thin as a boy, Ted sometimes was the object of ridicule and derision by the other boys because of his gawkiness. But he didn't mind. He could usually beat all the other boys at sports, particularly baseball.

Like many other sluggers—Babe Ruth included—Williams was primarily a pitcher in his first few years of baseball. Once he reached the majors, he made one pitching appearance for the Red Sox in 1940. But the painfully thin youngster was an extraordinary hitter even when pitching was his regular position. Swinging smoothly and seemingly without great effort from the left-handed side of the plate, Williams attracted legions of scouts to North Park and other San Diego playgrounds and athletic fields.

Once he discovered he had the potential to become a great hitter, hitting became Ted's life. He devoted all his time to improving his stroke, honing his skills, studying techniques of other batters and those of pitchers. In combination with the knowledge Williams acquired about hitting were the natural gifts with which he was endowed and which made it possible for him to apply the knowledge he gained. Ted had remarkable eyesight. It was said that he never swung at a pitch outside the strike zone. Other players told how umpires, in recognition of Ted's visual acumen, would call close pitches balls if Williams didn't offer at them. "If Ted didn't swing, it couldn't have been a good pitch," was the reasoning.

Williams still was swinging mostly at good pitches in 1960 when, though approaching forty-two years of age, he retained his unusually sharp pair of eyes. He also still possessed the good, quick wrists necessary for artful hitting. Ted couldn't run well any longer and fielding had become a difficult thing for him. But even during his peak years of athletic youth, Williams was no gazelle, and it often seemed that he spent time in leftfield, his regular position for many years, only because the rules required him to play in the field between turns at bat.

Downgrading the non-hitting aspects of Williams' play during his long career, as many Boston fans and journalists often did, always seemed analogous among outsiders to the old line, "All Bing Crosby can do is sing." With a hitter of Ted's magnitude, all else actually was secondary, since he could win so many ballgames just by swinging the bat. Williams, of course, recognized this. "All I want out of life," he once said, "is to be able to walk down the street and have people point to me and say, 'There goes the greatest hitter who ever lived.'"

There were many observers, press and fans alike, quite willing to accord that accolade to Ted as the 1960 season neared its conclusion and Williams prepared to leave the game. He had proved his point about wanting to play one more season. He erased the memory of his poor 1959 performance. In 1960, Ted was again a .300 hitter, closing the year with a .316 mark, as well as twenty-nine homers and seventy-two runs batted in.

The way the schedule fell, the Red Sox were slated to end the season on the road, at Yankee Stadium against the Bronx Bombers, who were en route to the World Series against the Pittsburgh Pirates. The Red Sox's last series of the year at Fenway Park came in the middle of the final week of the season against the surprising Baltimore Orioles, who had made a good run at the Yankees before falling back to second place.

The games meant nothing in the standings, but everyone in Boston knew that the third and final game of the series, scheduled for Wednesday afternoon, September 28, would be Williams' farewell to the home fans. Ted had made his retirement official a week before.

The day came up dark, dreary and drizzly in Boston. It was one of the worst days imaginable for a ballgame, cold and threatening. Only 10,454 fans turned out for Williams' last game in Boston. They had to see The Kid one more time. Johnny Orlando, the Red Sox clubhouse man, had labeled Ted "The Kid" many long years before.

In pre-game ceremonies at home plate, Curt Gowdy, the Boston television and radio broadcaster, described Williams as "controversial and colorful." Ted stood in the cold, dank stadium and said, "Despite some of the terrible things written about me by the newspapermen, my stay in Boston has been the most wonderful part of my life. If someone should ask me the one place I'd want to play if I had it do all over again, I would say Boston. It has the greatest owner in baseball and the greatest fans in America."

He didn't take batting practice but in the locker room before the game Williams was earnestly thinking about the manner in which he would go out. Unbeknownst to all but his teammates, the Red Sox manager Pinky Higgins, and club owner Yawkey, Ted had made a decision before the Baltimore series. Everyone realized it would be his last series in Boston. But Williams had decided it would be his last series, period. "Pinky, this is the last I'm going to play," he had told the manager. "I don't want to go to New York for those last couple of games. I want to finish up right here."

Having made this decision, Ted realized before the last game of the Baltimore series that he, in common with thousands of others before him, sincerely wanted to end on a dramatic note. Most players simply disappear from the lineup one day, and are forgotten quickly by the very fans who worshipped their every move when they were playing. Williams didn't want it to be that way, though his accomplishments had ruled out oblivion for him long before.

Steve Barber, a free-throwing left-hander, was the starting pitcher for the Orioles this cold, windy afternoon. Williams wasn't delighted with Barber's appearance. "He was very wild," said Ted later. "If I had had to bat against him four times that day, I might have gotten only one ball to hit all game."

But Barber was more than just usually wild this day. He faced five batters in the bottom of the first. He retired only one. He walked three, including Williams, the third batter, on four straight pitches, and hit catcher Jim Pagliaroni with a pitch. Barber also uncorked one wild pitch before he was mercifully removed by Orioles' manager Paul Richards in favor of right-hander Jack Fisher, a husky twenty-one-year-old product of Frostburg, Maryland.

Fisher, who had won twelve games for Baltimore, pitched strongly against the Red Sox. Boston had scored two runs off Barber in the first but were unable to score off Fisher through the seventh. Meanwhile, the Orioles had gone ahead, 4-2.

Williams got a couple of pitches he liked from Fisher and hit both well. One resulted in a flyball to rightcenter, which stayed up in the heavy atmosphere long enough for Jackie Brandt to catch it. In the fifth inning, Ted smacked the ball high and deep into the cloudy sky. It seemed headed for the rightfield stands, but at the last instant it died and landed in the glove of Al Pilarcik, who made the catch leaning against the sign that read three hundred and eighty feet. As he ran back to the dugout, Williams sighed to a teammate, "If that one didn't go out, none of them will today."

The wind was blowing in from rightfield to further dampen Williams' hope that he could drill a ball into the stands. The wind was much kinder to right-handed batters this day. Baltimore catcher Gus Triandos, who batted from the right side, had clubbed a homer in the second inning. But left-handers were having trouble.

Ted came up for what he figured was the last time in the eighth inning. By this time the Fenway Park lights had been turned on. Willie Tasby, the centerfielder, had led off for the Red Sox and had made out. Williams was the second man to face Fisher in the inning. Funny, he thought as he stepped in, this is going to be my last time at bat in baseball, and I'm forty-two years old and that kid pitcher out there is only twenty-one. He was born the same year I joined the Red Sox, 1939.

Fisher's first pitch was a ball. Then the Baltimore right-hander threw a sizzling fastball that Williams swung hard at but missed. Fisher, apparently sensing that Ted and all the fans in the stands wanted to settle quickly the matter of Williams' last major league at-bat, worked rapidly. He tried another fastball, throwing it just as hard as he had the previous one.

The Boston fans had been roaring cheers and pouring applause on Ted from the moment he had stepped to the plate in the eighth inning. Suddenly, as Fisher threw his third pitch, there was a hush from the stands. Williams swung and the ball took off on a diagonal line into centerfield. It seemed to fight the wind as it rose higher and farther into the deepest expanse of the field. Brandt ran back to the deepest corner of the outfield grass and made a mighty reach for the ball.

But it landed beyond the bullpen wall, four hundred and twenty feet from the point at which it made its initial contact. The crowd reacted as perhaps no crowd ever has reacted at a sports event. Though small in number, the fans let loose an ovation that resounded into the cold Boston atmosphere for several raucous minutes.

Ted circled the bases and ran into the dugout. Though the fans chanted for his reappearance on the field, in final acknowledgment of their cheers, Williams never returned, that day or any other day. Carroll Hardy replaced him in leftfield in the top of the ninth and the Red Sox staged a two-run rally in the bottom of the inning to win the game, 5-4.

But Williams' dramatic home run in his last at-bat was the major drama of the day once Ted informed the public, through the media, that the game had indeed been his last and that the eighth-inning home run off Fisher had been the last swing he would ever make in a major league uniform.

There was some disappointment that Williams had not made his decision known earlier. Possibly more hometown fans would have been attracted to attend his finale had they known it would actually be his finale. Furthermore, many fans in New York, always appreciative of Williams' incredible accomplishments, although they came in an enemy uniform, had looked forward to the privilege of bidding final farewell to Williams in the last two games of the entire season. Now they would never see Ted step to the plate again.

Williams, true to form, had angered and embittered some people over his last plate appearance in baseball. But no one ever can take away from him the thrill of hitting his final home run, the five hundred and twenty-first of his glorious career, on his very last opportunity.

Wednesday, September 28, 1960, at Boston

Baltimore	AB.	R.	H.	Boston	AB.	R.	H.
Brandt, cf	5	0	0	Green, ss	3	0	0
Pilarcik, rf	4	0	1	Tasby, cf	4	1	0
Robinson, 3b	4	1	1	WILLIAMS, lf	3	2	1
Gentile, 1b	3	1	1	Hardy, lf	0	0	0
Triandos, c	4	1	2	Pagliaroni, c	3	0	2
Hansen, ss	4	1	2	Malzone, 3b	3	0	0
Stephens, lf	4	0	2	Clinton, rf	3	0	0
Breeding, 2b	2	0	0	Gile, 1b	4	0	0
aWoodling	1	0	0	Coughtry, 2b	3	1	2
bPearson	0	0	0	Muffett, p	2	0	0
Klaus, 2b	1	0	0	aNixon	1	0	0
Barber, p	0	0	0	Fornieles, p	0	0	0
Fisher, p	4	0	0	bWertz	1	0	1
	—	—	—	eBrewer	0	1	0
Totals	36	4	9		—	—	—
				Totals	30	5	6

aHit into force play for Breeding in sixth
bRan for Woodling in sixth
cGrounded into double play for Muffett in seventh
dDoubled for Fornieles in ninth
eRan for Wertz in ninth

| Baltimore | 0 2 0 | 0 1 1 | 0 0 0—4 |
| Boston | 2 0 0 | 0 0 0 | 0 1 2—5 |

Two out when winning run was scored

Error—Coughtry, Klaus. Runs batted in—Gentile, Triandos 2, Woodling, Tasby, Williams, Clinton. Double plays—Klaus, Hansen and Gentile. Left on base—Baltimore 6, Boston 7. Two-base hits—Stephens, Robinson, Wertz. Home runs—Triandos, Williams. Sacrifice fly—Clinton, Gentile.

	IP.	H.	R.	ER.	BB.	SO.
Barber	1/3	0	2	2	3	0
Fisher (L, 12-11)	8 1/3	6	3	2	3	5
Muffett	7	9	4	4	0	4
Fornieles (W, 10-5)	2	0	0	0	0	2

Hit by pitcher—by Barber (Pagliaroni). Wild pitch—Barber, Muffett. Umpires—Hurley, Rice, Stevens, Drummond. Time—2:18. Attendance—10,454.

Roger Maris—One More Than Ruth

The trouble with a team's clinching its league pennant too early is that it often must play before empty stadiums for the remainder of the regular league schedule. Even the most zealous supporters of a team find it difficult to muster the necessary enthusiasm to attend games in late September when the manager may be resting his regulars or giving them brief workouts at best to keep them fit for the upcoming World Series.

When the New York Yankees were running roughshod over the rest of the American League for years, they often had the pennant wrapped up in the early days of September. To be frank, there were some seasons when they could have hung the pennant over Yankee Stadium by the end of April.

But 1961 was different for the Yankees. Though they had settled the matter of the American League championship by a convincing margin over second-place Detroit as the season droned into its final few days, the Yankees still held the interest of a tremendous number of fans. The interest wasn't confined merely to partisans of the Bronx Bombers. The rapture for the late-season doings of the '61 Yankees was nationwide.

The reason was left-hand-hitting New York outfielder Roger Maris. Going into the last day of regular play, Maris, the twenty-seven-year-old blond-haired product of Fargo, North Dakota, had hit exactly sixty home runs in 1961. This tied Maris with Babe Ruth for the most homers ever hit by a player in a single major league season.

Roger had tied the Babe at sixty homers with a blast off Jack Fisher of the Baltimore Orioles on September 26 in a night game at Yankee Stadium. In three games since then he had failed to hit a home run. Now it was Sunday, October 1, Maris' last chance to surpass Ruth. Could he make it?

This was the question in the minds of the 23,154 fans who paid their way into Yankee Stadium for the Sunday afternoon contest. The Boston Red Sox would provide the opposition in the Yankees' final tuneup before the start of the World Series three days later against the National league champion Cincinnati Reds. Yankee manager Ralph Houk, in his first year at the helm after replacing Casey Stengel as the club's field boss, already had announced that he would juggle his lineup all afternoon to give as many players as possible a last day's workout.

Houk also announced that Maris would remain in the game all the way to assure him enough plate appearances for a shot at his sixty-first home run. With Mickey Mantle, New York's slugging centerfielder, resting his constantly aching knees on this final Sunday of the season, Roger got a rare start in the middle of the outfield, moving over from his customary station in rightfield. Though Houk didn't move Maris to centerfield for any particular effect, there was tremendous irony in the fact that Roger's final game of 1961 should be played in centerfield. Irony, because for much of the season both Maris and Mantle had fought on virtually even terms to be the first to dethrone Ruth as the single-season home run king.

As the favorite and darling of the Yankee team and fans, Mantle was the popular choice to reach sixty-one homers, if anyone reached it at all. Roger sensed that most people thought Mickey would surpass Ruth and that he, Maris, would fall short. Roger also realized that even Yankee fans resented his encroachment on Ruth's mark, one of the most revered in baseball, because he had not been an original Yankee product, nurtured, like Mantle, in the Yankee farm system. Maris had begun his major league career with the Cleveland Indians in 1957, had been traded to the Kansas City Athletics in 1958, and had joined the Yankees in 1960.

It wasn't easy for Roger to accept the fact that even people who should have been among his loyal backers, Yankee fans, openly rooted for him *not* to surpass Babe Ruth, but shouted themselves hoarse every time Mantle connected. For much of the year, the two slugging outfielders kept apace in home run blasts. They became the first twosome from one team ever to hit more than fifty homers each. But Mantle reached fifty-four homers and then stopped. Maris went past fifty-four on September 7, and kept clouting baseballs into the stands as September ran its course. With each succeeding home run, with each advancing step by Maris toward Ruth's record, the pressure mounted on the North Dakotan.

One could feel, virtually hold, the pressure that gripped Yankee Stadium before the final game of the 1961 season. Practically everyone in the stands was there for only one purpose: to see Maris go after Ruth's record. Nothing else was of interest to anyone.

Among those who wondered whether Roger could hit number sixty-one was Mrs. Babe Ruth, widow of the famous Sultan of Swat. She sat in the box seat near the Yankee dugout in which she usually could be found during all major events at Yankee Stadium, oldtimers' games, "days" for ballplayers and the like.

Many of the fans gathered in clusters in the rightfield stands, in the vicinity of the foul pole. This was one of Maris' favorite home run areas. A sportswriter brought his glove to the ballpark and sat among the fans in the rightfield stands. What a story he would have if he should catch a ball hit by Maris for his sixty-first homer! Even the girls in the stands carried baseball gloves. The Yankee bullpen crew, located directly in front of the stands, also was alert. Many ballplayers like to pretend they do not become emotionally involved in record performances, their own or those of others. But the Yankees working in the bullpen this October afternoon were grateful for their excellent vantage point should Roger hit one out there.

The 1961 Red Sox were a nondescript group. Win or lose this final Sunday, they were destined to a sixth-place finish in the ten-team league. The American circuit had grown from eight to ten clubs with the addition of teams in Los Angeles and the Twin Cities of Minneapolis-St. Paul.

Tracy Stallard was the choice of Boston manager Pinky Higgins to start the last game of the year. Stallard was a twenty-four-year-old right-hander from Coeburn, in the Virginia hills. He stood six feet, five inches tall and threw a good fastball and a sharp-breaking curve. He was just getting started in the majors that 1961 season, and he had won two games while making infrequent appearances.

Stallard knew the importance of pitching in this game. If he kept Maris from reaching his goal of sixty-one home runs, he would gain fame and notoriety for sure. If, on the other hand, he yielded a home run pitch to Maris—well, he would be famous and notorious for that too. No one who follows baseball ever has forgotten the name of Tom Zachary, a Washington Senators' pitcher of the nineteen-twenties. Zachary's name has survived, and will continue to survive down through the ages, because he was the pitcher who served up Ruth's sixtieth home run in 1927. So Stallard stood to be remembered either way, as the man who stopped the mighty Maris or as the victim of his record-smashing home run.

The tall young right-hander could have taken the safe route. He could have thrown Maris an endless series of bad pitches, forcing Roger to go chasing pitches out of the strike zone rather than accept walks. But to his credit, Stallard played the game straight. Maris later acknowledged this with gratitude.

"I appreciate the guy was man enough to pitch to me to get me out," Roger said.

In his first time at bat in the bottom of the first inning, Maris hit the ball well to leftfield, his opposite field. But it was short of the stands and was hauled in for the out by the leftfielder. The Red Sox leftfielder was a rookie named Carl Yastrzemski, who had replaced the immortal Ted Williams in the Boston lineup following Williams' retirement.

Neither the Yankees nor the Red Sox were doing much hitting and Maris had a long wait before his second turn at bat came around. By edict of the Commissioner of Baseball, Ford C. Frick, Roger already had taken too long to reach the point where he was threatening to surpass Babe Ruth.

Though Maris started 1961 slowly with only four homers in the first twenty-nine games of the season, he caught fire in May and June, and remained ablaze through July. By the end of July, Roger already had reached the forty home run mark.

It was about this time that the arguments began developing about Babe Ruth's record of sixty home runs in one year. The biggest argument ran that even if Maris did hit sixty home runs or more (he was three weeks ahead of Ruth's 1927 pace at this time), he would have to do it within one hundred and fifty-four games, as Ruth had, or it shouldn't count.

Others countered by arguing that a record is a record, regardless of details. When the fiberglass pole for pole-vaulting was developed in the nineteen-sixties, every pole vault record in the track and field books was broken countless times. Today's pole vaulters climb eighteen feet into the sky with the fiberglass pole. The vaulters of the past, who used poles made of bamboo, aluminum or other substances, may have been as skilled as the modern vaulters. But that does not change the fact that the eighteen-foot vaulters of today are credited with the world records.

Working behind the scenes in the Ruth-Maris home run dispute was a propaganda group that made no secret of its intention to keep the Babe's record alive and intact, somehow, some way, at any cost. Commissioner Frick finally yielded to pressures and ruled that Ruth's record would have to be broken, by Maris, Mantle or anybody else, in one hundred and fifty-four games or less. Otherwise Ruth's record would continue to be listed in the official tomes of baseball.

Frick didn't actually say that an asterisk would precede the name of the player who surpassed Ruth if it took him more than one hundred and fifty-four games. But that is precisely what happened. If you examine the official records now, you'll find parentheses which hold the words, "162-game season," next to the name of the man who hit one more homer than Ruth.

For all his home runs, Maris did not consider himself a superstar. He didn't have the batting average of a superstar. He was to close out the 1961 season as a .269 hitter. Roger was a fine all-round player, though, with excellent skills in the outfield—speed, fielding range, strong throwing arm—as well as his propensity for hitting baseballs great distances.

Maris probably would not have chosen to be a home run hitter of Ruthian proportions if the decision had been left to him. He did not seek fame, but it had been thrust upon him by fate. He didn't always handle it well, feuding with reporters and, at times, other members of the Yankees.

But Roger couldn't stop hitting home runs. When he hit his fiftieth, off Ken McBride of the Los Angeles Angels, making him the ninth player ever to hit that many in a season, Maris attempted to explain the turmoil his prodigious hitting was causing within him. "I never wanted all this hoopla," Roger said. "All I wanted was to be a good ballplayer, to hit twenty-five or thirty homers, drive in around a hundred runs, hit .280 and help whatever team I was on win pennants. I just wanted to be one of the guys, an average guy having a good season."

Instead the spotlight glared on him mercilessly, as it did when the one-hundred-and-fifty-four game mark neared and Roger needed two homers to tie Ruth within the stipulated time to earn himself the official record. Actually it was New York's one hundred and fifty-fifth game of the year. There had been a tie game early in the season. And Maris actually had hit his fifty-ninth earlier in the season, at Baltimore in July. But that homer was washed off the books when rain forced cancellation of the game before it became official.

In his last chance to match Ruth within the one-hundred-and-fifty-four game requirement, Maris gave one of the most courageous performances any player ever gave. In his five times at bat, Roger hit five long drives against the Baltimore Orioles. Two were caught in the deepest reaches of the outfield in Baltimore Memorial Stadium, one of the biggest stadiums in baseball. Two other long drives by Maris curved foul into the rightfield stands.

The fifth long drive was Roger's fifty-ninth homer, off Milt Pappas in the third inning. But he couldn't reach the magic number sixty that night. He had some consolation in the fact that the Yankees clinched their second straight American League pennant by beating the Orioles.

Now it was time for Maris to step in for his second time at bat against Tracy Stallard on October 1. Roger's fifty-ninth and sixtieth homers had been hit in his second plate appearance of those games. Would this again be his time to strike?

Stallard's first pitch to Roger was high and outside for ball one. The next delivery from the tall right-hander was low and a bit inside. Another ball. Now Maris was ahead on the count, two balls and no strikes. He took a few quick practice swings as Stallard leaned over to get the sign from his catcher, Russ Nixon, for the third pitch.

Stallard threw a fastball about waist high. Maris swung and the ball leapt from his bat. Catcher Elston Howard, in the Yankee dugout, shouted, "That's it!" The ball landed in the lower deck of the rightfield stands, to the right of the bullpen and about six rows back. As the crowd yelled itself hoarse for baseball's new home run king, Maris had only one thought. "I was so happy I wasn't paying any attention to what was going on," he later admitted. "I just wanted to get around the bases, touch each one and make it count."

After Maris' record-setting home run, the rest of the afternoon was anticlimactic. In his last two times at bat Roger struck out and popped out to second. His home run proved to be the only run of the game, and the Yankees scored their one hundred and ninth victory of the season, 1-0.

After the game Maris posed with a young man from Brooklyn who had caught the historic home run blast. The boy's name was Sal Durante. Sal didn't keep the ball very long. A restaurant owner who had flown all the way from Sacramento, California, to view the historic sports moment, presented Durante with a check for $5000 for the ball. The restaurant man didn't want the ball for himself. He offered the $5000 to make certain that the famous ball would be returned to Maris. As soon as Sal Durante turned over the ball for the $5000 check, the restaurant owner presented it to Roger.

When he was a boy in Fargo, Roger Eugene Maris thought any trophies he might one day receive for sports would be for his prowess in football. Shanley High School in Fargo, which Roger attended, had no baseball team, so young Maris played during the summer in midget leagues and later in the American Legion.

Shanley did have other sports, and Roger played most of them. He excelled in basketball and at track, but football was his best sport. Twice he was named an all-state halfback at Shanley, and he led the state in scoring in his senior year. Born on September 10, 1934, Maris graduated from high school in June, 1953, and was deluged by college scholarship offers for football. The most attractive offer came from the University of Oklahoma, one of the great national powers in intercollegiate football.

Roger considered the football scholarship offers seriously. But when a scout from the Cleveland Indians, Frank Fahey, invited him to come to Cleveland to show what he could do in baseball, Maris went. The Indians liked what they saw and offered Maris a $15,000 bonus and promised that, if Roger signed, he would be sent to a farm team near his home—the Fargo-Moorehead club in the Northern League. That's where Roger first played professional baseball.

Eventually promoted to the Indians in 1957, Maris didn't produce as he had been expected to and was dealt to Kansas City the following year. The A's were a weak club and Roger turned out to be more valuable to them as trading material than as a potential regular. At the end of the 1959 season the A's dangled Maris' name around both leagues as a player they would like to trade. The Pittsburgh Pirates were interested. As part of the deal by which Maris would come to Pittsburgh, the Pirates were prepared to send Dick Groat, their regular shortstop, to Kansas City.

Finally, that deal fell through and Maris was traded to the Yankees instead. In 1960, he hit thirty-nine homers and was named the American League's Most Valuable Player in his first season in New York livery. The man for whom he almost had seen sent to Pittsburgh, Dick Groat, won the National League's MVP honor as the Pirates won the National League flag and then triumphed over the Yankees in the seven-game World Series of 1960.

Wouldn't the entire pattern of baseball history have looked quite different if that Maris-for-Groat deal ever had been completed in 1960? Quite possibly, there might never have been a man who could hit sixty-one home runs in a single major league season.

Sunday, October 1, 1961, at Yankee Stadium, New York

Boston	AB.	R.	H.
Schilling, 2b	4	0	1
Geiger, cf	4	0	0
Yastrzemski, lf	4	0	1
Malzone, 3b	4	0	0
Clinton, rf	4	0	0
Runnels, 1b	3	0	0
Gile, 1b	0	0	0
Nixon, c	3	0	2
Green, ss	2	0	0
Stallard, p	1	0	0
bJensen	1	0	0
Nichols, p	0	0	0
Totals	30	0	4

New York	AB.	R.	H.
Richardson, 2b	4	0	0
Kubek, ss	4	0	2
MARIS, cf	4	1	1
Berra, lf	2	0	0
Lopez, lf-rf	1	0	0
Blanchard, rf-c	3	0	0
Howard, c	2	0	0
Reed, lf	1	0	1
Skowron, 1b	2	0	0
Hale, 1b	1	0	1
Boyer, 3b	2	0	0
Stafford, p	2	0	0
Reniff, p	0	0	0
aTresh	1	0	0
Arroyo, p	0	0	0
Totals	29	1	5

aPopped up for Reniff in seventh
bPopped up for Stallard in eighth

Boston	0 0 0	0 0 0	0 0 0—0
New York	0 0 0	1 0 0	0 0 x—1

Error—None. Left on base—Boston 5, New York 5. Run batted in—Maris. Triple—Nixon. Home run—Maris. Stolen base—Geiger. Sacrifice—Stallard.

	IP.	H.	R.	ER.	BB.	SO.
Stallard (L, 2-7)	7	5	1	1	1	5
Nichols	1	0	0	0	0	0
Stafford (W, 14-9)	6	3	0	0	1	7
Reniff	1	0	0	0	0	1
Arroyo	2	1	0	0	0	1

Wild pitch—Stallard. Passed ball—Nixon. Umpires—Kinnamon, Flaherty, Honochick and Salerno. Time—1:51. Attendance—23,154.

Sandy Koufax—The Perfect Pitcher

During the last five seasons of his career with the Los Angeles Dodgers, Sandy Koufax pitched many important games for the team. In fact, probably no one in baseball was called upon as frequently in clutch situations as was the Brooklyn-born left-hander during the years he rated as the best pitcher of his time. Many experts maintained that the southpaw wearing Dodger uniform number 32 was the best pitcher of any time.

With the possible exception of the World Series games in which he pitched, perhaps no game Sandy worked was as crucial as the one in which the Dodgers faced the Chicago Cubs on Thursday night, September 9, 1965, at Dodger Stadium in Chavez Ravine.

As he took his warmup pitches prior to facing the Cubs, Koufax realized that a great deal was riding on the outcome. For one thing, with just three weeks remaining in the regular season, the Dodgers were tied for second place in the National League with Cincinnati, half a game behind the San Francisco Giants. Every game played by Los Angeles, Cincinnati and San Francisco could now be considered critical.

Secondly, Sandy was in the midst of an uncommon slump. Though he already had captured twenty-one victories against only seven defeats, three of those setbacks had come in his most recent four starts, two by one-run margins. Though, by the standards of most pitchers, Koufax was firing his fastball and curve with his usual precision, the thirty-year-old southpaw wasn't most pitchers; he was *the* pitcher of his era, the most celebrated hurler in the nation.

Logically, Sandy Koufax should have been unable to throw a baseball at all in 1965. On August 8 of the previous season, 1964, Sandy was victimized by his constant nemesis, the injury jinx. The 1964 season saw a tremendous tumble by the Dodgers after their four-game World Series sweep over the New York Yankees in '63. Koufax wasn't one of those Dodgers who collapsed in 1964. Before August 8, in fact, he had won fifteen of his sixteen most recent decisions.

But on the fateful day he slid hard into second base and landed on his left elbow. It was an irony indeed that a great pitcher like Koufax should be injured on the bases, a portion of the playing field Sandy rarely saw up close. Koufax was perhaps the worst hitter who ever played in the major leagues. His negative batting statistics were almost on a level of uniqueness with his awesome pitching records. One year Sandy was retired every time he came to bat—and each out was a strikeout!

Koufax tried to pitch after falling on his elbow. He tried for several weeks. But the pain was so severe that he finally went to see Dr. Robert Kerlan, the team physician of the Dodgers. At that time Sandy had no way of knowing that the slide on which he injured himself had begun the arthritic condition in his elbow that would cut short his brilliant career after the 1966 season when he was not quite thirty-one.

Dr. Kerlan advised Koufax to forget pitching for the remainder of the 1964 season, hoping that rest and treatment would combine to make the arm sound for the beginning of the 1965 campaign.

For the first three weeks of spring training in 1965, Sandy was able to pitch with no pain. But constant work caused the elbow to flare up. Finally Dr. Kerlan decided that the only way to prevent the constant swelling was to give Sandy a shot in the elbow every time he pitched. Then, as soon as Koufax was through with a game, he was to put on a rubber sleeve and submerge the arm in a tub of ice water.

The measures prescribed by Dr. Kerlan were successful. By August 10, 1965, Sandy had won twenty games and lost only four. Everyone in the National League knew that there was something wrong with Koufax's arm, but his performances didn't reflect any problems. "Some sore elbow," said Cincinnati manager Dick Sisler one day. "It's sore except between the first and ninth innings of ballgames."

In jest, Sisler actually was quite correct. Each time that Sandy was scheduled to pitch, Dr. Kerlan was able to arrest the arthritis long enough for Sandy to work a game. With shots and medication and dunks of his elbow into the ice water, Sandy could pitch every fourth day without pain and without swelling. For the three days between his starts, Sandy felt pain, agonizing pain, and had swelling.

But, typically, Koufax pushed himself virtually to the outer limits of his pain threshold in order to keep the Dodgers in what proved to be a ferociously fought 1965 pennant race.

Now it was September 9, and each game could mean precious points or lengths in the National League standings. The Dodgers were hoping desperately that Sandy could pull out of his losing slump and get them on the winning path toward the pennant.

Actually, Sandy's slump was more attributable to the impotent Los Angeles bats than to any decline in his pitching skills. The Dodgers of 1965 were a team virtually devoid of offensive weaponry, the kind that drives baseballs over buildings and opposing managers to drink. A big inning for the '65 Dodgers consisted of a walk to shortstop Maury Wills, a steal of second by Wills, a sacrifice bunt to send Wills to third, and a fly ball to drive him home.

People in Los Angeles used to kid Koufax that, in order for him to win, he practically had to pitch a shut-out or a no-hit game. Sandy had prepared for this eventuality by tossing a no-hitter in each of the three previous seasons, in 1962 against the New York Mets, in 1963 against the San Francisco Giants and in 1964 against the Philadelphia Phillies. Against the Phillies, Sandy had allowed only one man to reach first base. That was Richie Allen, via a walk. "I changed my mind about what to throw him during the windup," Sandy later recalled. "It was a 3-2 pitch and I ended up throwing it low. I might have gotten Allen out if I had gone ahead and thrown what I was going to throw originally."

In all of baseball, only three other pitchers—Larry Corcoran, Cy Young and Bob Feller—ever had pitched three no-hitters. And of the three, only Feller before Sandy had pitched all three of his masterpieces in the twentieth century.

There were 29,139 fans in Dodger Stadium to watch Koufax pitch against the Chicago Cubs on September 9, 1965. Sandy's pitching opponent was another hard-throwing left-hander, twenty-six-year-old Bob Hendley, from Macon, Georgia. Hendley had come to the Cubs earlier in 1965 from the San Francisco Giants.

For four innings, neither Koufax nor Hendley allowed a hit. In the fifth, the Dodgers put on one of their typical offensive displays. They scored a run without getting a hit. Lou Johnson, Los Angeles' leftfielder, walked, was sacrificed to second, stole third and continued home when catcher Chris Krug threw wildly past third base.

Both sides still were hitless until the seventh inning. For a while, the Dodger Stadium fans thought they might be witnessing the second double no-hit game in baseball history. On May 2, 1917, Fred Toney of the Cincinnati Reds and Jim "Hippo" Vaughn of Chicago pitched nine hitless innings against each other, until the Reds finally broke through against Vaughn in the tenth and won the game, 1-0.

Koufax retired all three Cub batters in the top of the seventh, and through seven innings had set down all twenty-one men he had faced. Billy Williams, the third Chicago out of the seventh, was retired on an easy fly ball to leftfielder Johnson. It was the last time any of the Dodger fielders saw the ball all evening.

In the Los Angeles half of the seventh, Johnson, who had scored the only run of the game in the fifth, broke through with the game's first hit—a bloop double. But the Dodgers couldn't stand success. They couldn't get another man on base in the inning.

When Koufax went to the mound for the top of the eighth inning, the fans in Dodger Stadium were buzzing excitedly. Could Sandy keep up his perfect pitching? The game had begun as an important contest in the pennant race but now was much more than that.

Ron Santo, the hard-hitting third baseman of the Cubs, was the first Chicago batter in the eighth. He was called out on strikes. Then came "Mr. Cub," Ernie Banks. He fanned, and so did Byron Browne, to the uproarious approval of the 29,139 fans. Now dandy Sandy was only three outs away from perfection.

In the ninth Koufax carried his slim 1-0 lead to the mound. Not only was Sandy within reach of one of baseball's rarest achievements, but he also had to be concerned that, if one pitch were grooved too finely, a Cub batsman could wallop the ball into the stands for a home run and tie the score.

Catcher Chris Krug was Chicago's first batter in the

ninth. He was desperately seeking to make amends for his error that had given the Dodgers the only score of the game in the fifth inning. But Sandy smoked Krug out of the box with three blazing fastballs. Having relied on his curveballs in the early innings, Koufax now called almost exclusively on his high, hard one.

Sandy threw three straight fastballs to Joey Amalfitano, pinch-hitting for shortstop Don Kessinger. Amalfitano swung at all three pitches and missed them all.

Harvey Kuenn, a veteran hitter with many .300 seasons behind him in the American League, was the next man at the plate. He was batting in place of Hendley, who stood on the verge of losing a game in which he had yielded only one bloop hit and an unearned run.

Kuenn was not an easy man to retire in these situations, or, for that matter, in any situation. He knew how to get enough of a piece of the ball to cause a pitcher to waste several pitches to him. Then, with the pitcher in the hole and having to come in with a good one, Kuenn could drop a single almost anywhere in the ballpark.

For a moment, Koufax thought of going back to his breaking pitches against Kuenn. Then he thought better of it. His fastball was so effective, so quick, there seemed little point in abandoning it now. Sandy threw three fastballs to Kuenn. Kuenn probably still hasn't seen any of them. He swung in vain at all three pitches and didn't come close. Koufax had a record-setting fourth no-hitter and he had made it a perfect game, only the ninth on record. By striking out the last six batters, he ended the game with fourteen strikeouts, en route to establishing a one-season record of 382 strikeouts by the end of the 1965 season.

Sandy Koufax, king of the southpaws, was born Sanford Braun on December 30, 1935. In later years, a writer would suggest, pointing to Sandy's Jewish background, that his date of birth, December 30, be added to the list of Jewish religious holidays.

Sandy's father, Jack Braun, was an athletic man from whom Sandy inherited his size and strength. When he pitched in the big leagues Sandy stood six feet, two inches and weighed 210 pounds.

When Sandy was eleven years old, his parents, Jack and Evelyn Braun, were divorced. His mother was remarried, to an attorney named Irving Koufax, who adopted Sandy and gave him his name.

Sandy's favorite sport as a boy was basketball, and he ultimately earned a college basketball scholarship to the University of Cincinnati, where he spent one year. Baseball was something to play between basketball seasons. He played infrequently, without much interest, and as likely as not, at almost any position but pitcher.

The man who first spotted young Koufax as a potential baseball player was Milton Laurie, who drove a delivery truck for the New York *Journal-American,* a newspaper now defunct.

"I first saw Sandy with a team called the Tomahawks in the Ice Cream League in Brooklyn," recalled Laurie, a long-time sandlot manager in New York. "I saw him pitch and he walked nine men in two innings, but I tried to get him on my team. He refused, saying basketball was his game. When I saw him playing first base at Lafayette High School and throwing bullets across the infield, I begged him again. Finally he joined us. But he worked in camps during the summer and didn't pitch much. But, boy, when he did—sixteen, eighteen strikeouts every game."

Even after he had forsaken basketball for good and devoted all his attention to pitching big league ball, Sandy was liable to strike out every batter he faced— or at least those he didn't walk. Koufax signed with the Dodgers in 1955, when the team still was based in Brooklyn. For his first six years as a Dodger, three in Brooklyn and three in Los Angeles, Sandy tantalized the club management with an occasional brilliant effort, such as eighteen strikeouts in a game against the San Francisco Giants in 1959, tying the existing record. But then Sandy would lapse into mediocrity again, as quickly as he had emerged.

Koufax finally found the secret to pitching success in 1961 spring training in Florida. Sandy was throwing a few pitches easily to catcher Norm Sherry one day, when Sherry noticed something. "You know, Sandy, you're not throwing as hard as you usually do, with the big motion and everything," Sherry told Koufax. "But the ball is landing in my glove just as hard and just as fast as it does when you give it the big windup. Why don't you try throwing with the same easy, relaxed motion in the games?"

Koufax listened to Sherry's advice, tried it in a couple games, and soon was on his way. Sandy had considered retiring from baseball because his lack of success had become such a frustration to him. Instead, he won eighteen games in 1961 and vaulted into the upper echelon of big league pitchers. From that point through 1966, when his arthritic condition forced him to retire, Koufax was the dominant pitcher in the game.

Sandy always gave his best effort, even when he was called on to pitch batting practice to the Dodgers. A teammate once stepped out of the batter's cage after futilely trying to hit several of Koufax's offerings and announced, "Taking batting practice against him is like playing Russian roulette with five bullets. You don't give yourself much of a chance."

Imagine how batters on opposing teams must have felt when they faced Koufax.

Here's how Sandy Koufax retired twenty-seven consecutive Chicago Cubs' batters in his perfect game:

First Inning—Don Young popped to the second baseman. Glenn Beckert struck out. Billy Williams was called out on strikes.

Second Inning—Ron Santo fouled to the catcher. Ernie Banks struck out. Byron Browne lined to center.

Third Inning—Chris Krug flied to center. Don Kessinger flied to right. Bob Hendley was called out on strikes.

Fourth Inning—Young fouled out to first. Beckert flied to right. Williams was called out on strikes.

Fifth Inning—Santo flied to left. Banks struck out. Browne grounded to second.

Sixth Inning—Krug grounded to second. Kessinger grounded to third. Hendley struck out.

Seventh Inning—Young struck out. Beckert flied to right. Williams flied to left.

Eighth Inning—Santo was called out on strikes. Banks struck out. Browne struck out.

Ninth Inning—Krug struck out. Joe Amalfitano, batting for Kessinger, struck out, Harvey Kuenn, batting for Hendley, struck out.

Thursday, September 9, 1965, at Los Angeles

Chicago	AB.	R.	H.	Los Angeles	AB.	R.	H.
Young, cf	3	0	0	Wills, ss	3	0	0
Beckert, 2b	3	0	0	Gilliam, 3b	3	0	0
Williams, rf	3	0	0	W. Davis, cf	3	0	0
Santo, 3b	3	0	0	Johnson, lf	2	1	1
Banks, 1b	3	0	0	Fairly, rf	2	0	0
Browne, lf	3	0	0	Lefebvre, 2b	3	0	0
Krug, c	3	0	0	Tracewski, 2b	0	0	0
Kessinger, ss	2	0	0	Parker, 1b	3	0	0
aAmalfitano	1	0	0	Torborg, c	3	0	0
Hendley, p	2	0	0	KOUFAX, p	2	0	0
bKuenn	1	0	0				
Totals	27	0	0	Totals	24	1	1

```
Chicago ............................ 0 0 0   0 0 0   0 0 0—0
Los Angeles ....................... 0 0 0   0 1 0   0 0 x—1
```

aStruck out for Kessinger in ninth. bStruck out for Hendley in ninth. Run batted in—None. Two-base hit—Johnson. Sacrifice hit—Fairly. Stolen base—Johnson. Left on bases—Los Angeles 1, Chicago 0. Bases on balls—Off Hendley 1 (Johnson). Strikeouts—By KOUFAX 14 (Young, Beckert, Williams 2, Santo, Banks 3, Browne, Krug, Amalfitano, Hendley 2, Kuenn), by Hendley 3 (Lefebvre 2, KOUFAX). Runs and earned runs—Off Hendley 1-0. Winning pitcher—KOUFAX (22-7). Losing pitcher—Hendley (2-3). Umpires—Vargo, Pelekoudas, Jackowski and Pryor. Time—1:43. Attendance—29,139.

Bob Gibson—Series Strikeout King

When a boy named Robert Gibson was born in Omaha, Nebraska, on November 9, 1935, no father came to take him and his mother home from the hospital. The father of the boy had died three months before the boy was born, leaving the mother to support her seven children alone.

The mother had to work long hours in a laundry to make enough money to take care of her large family. This didn't always leave her enough time to look after her children's need for companionship and advice. Josh, the oldest boy, was fifteen years old and, in the absence of a real father for the other children, Josh served as a father-figure. No one needed Josh more than the youngest Gibson boy, Robert, who was called Bob.

Bob was a sickly youngster. While still very young, he was stricken with pneumonia, the same disease that killed his father. Living conditions in Omaha's North Side ghetto were poor, to say the least, and it was relatively simple for a boy with no parental guidance on health matters to become ill. But Bob was an unusually sick boy, even by the standards of his environment.

After he recovered from pneumonia, the youngest Gibson boy fell victim to a variety of other ailments. He suffered from rickets, hay fever, asthma and a rheumatic heart.

The boy conquered all these ailments and grew up big and strong, with the help of his big brother Josh, who introduced him to sports. As he grew older Bob overcame his early infirmities and developed into a solidly built athlete. At Omaha Technical High School, he won letters in three sports—baseball, basketball and track. Once a scrawny, frail boy, Bob had grown to six feet, one inch and 190 pounds.

Bob won an athletic scholarship to Creighton University, located in his hometown of Omaha. At Creighton he starred in baseball and basketball, and attracted the attention of professional scouts in both sports. Bill Bergesch was general manager of the Omaha professional baseball team, which was a farm club for the St. Louis Cardinals. He knew Bob's brother Josh very well, having supplied the city recreation department, where Josh worked, with baseball equipment over the years. In his senior year at Creighton, Bob worked out for Bergesch and Johnny Keane, the field manager of the Omaha club. Both men liked what they saw and signed him to a pro contract with the Cardinals.

By 1959, Gibson was up with the Cardinals, to stay, he thought. In his first start, he shut out the Cincinnati Reds, 1-0.

But Bob shuttled between the majors and minors for a couple of seasons, never achieving any consistency. In July, 1961, Keane, Bob's manager at Omaha, took the reins of the St. Louis club and Gibson began to thrive. He had chafed from the heat of the often stinging criticism of deposed Cardinal manager Solly Hemus. Under Keane, Gibson became a star.

There was no greater pitching star in the major leagues in the late 1960s than Bob Gibson, the once sickly boy from the Omaha ghetto. Few hurlers in all the years of baseball history have put together the kind of records that Gibson compiled for the Cardinals, particularly during St. Louis' pennant-winning years of 1967-68.

Though he was sidelined by a broken leg for much of the latter part of the 1967 regular season, Bob was ready to return to action when the World Series rolled around. The Cardinals faced the Boston Red Sox for baseball's most coveted prize, the world title, and Gibson was the difference. He won three games in three starts, all complete games, including a 7-2 victory in the seventh and decisive game. Bob twirled a five-hit, 6-0 shutout in the fourth game.

But Gibson, as it turned out, was just warming up his powerful right arm. The arm ultimately was to establish a major league record for the most seasons over 200 strikeouts. Bob achieved it in eight years.

Probably no pitcher ever has enjoyed the kind of season Gibson enjoyed in 1968. He had carried the nickname, "Hoot" since his minor league days in Omaha, after the Western star of silent motion picture days, Hoot Gibson. No pistol-packing gunslinger ever was more dangerous with his weapon than was Gibson with a baseball in his hands in 1968.

It didn't begin as an auspicious year either for Bob or for the Cardinals. The defending world champions were not acting like defending champions. They showed a pitiful inability to score runs. Gibson was pitching brilliantly almost every time out, but had little to show for it. After nine starts, he owned a glittering 1.33 earned-run average, the best in the majors, but his won-lost mark was only 3-4. During his nine starts, Bob had been backed up by only eleven runs! During the same period Bob had yielded merely twelve earned runs.

On June 2, Gibson beat the New York Mets, 6-3. That began an incredible winning streak of fifteen games that didn't end until the Pittsburgh Pirates beat him on August 24, 6-4, with the not inconsiderable help of three unearned runs. At one point during his long undefeated skein, Bob hurled five consecutive shutouts, one short of the major league record set by Don Drysdale of the Los Angeles Dodgers.

Gibson's attempt for a sixth straight shutout came against the Dodgers. But it ended quickly when Bob wild-pitched a run home in the first inning. It was the only run he allowed as he went on to a 3-1 triumph. In the locker room after the game, Bob was light-hearted about the manner in which his scoreless streak had been broken. When a reporter asked him if the pressure of the streak had gotten to him and caused him to throw the wild pitch that let in the Dodger run, Gibson laughed.

"Pressure?" Bob chuckled. "Call it aggravation. I could never feel any pressure again after the pressure I had growing up in Omaha."

Even when Bob's long winning streak was broken, he gave a brilliant performance. He struck out fifteen Pittsburgh batters in the game in which the Pirates beat him to end the unbeaten skein. Someone later figured out that, during his fifteen-game stretch without a defeat, Gibson allowed the unbelievably low yield of seven earned runs and tossed ten shutouts en route.

Before the season drew to a close with the Cardinals winning their second National League pennant in a row, Bob pitched three more shutouts for a total of thirteen for the season, one of the highest totals ever recorded in a single year.

But that wasn't all. Also included in Gibson's final won-lost mark of 22-9 were twenty-eight complete games in thirty-four starts, a league high of 268 strike-outs, and the most incredible statistic of all, an earned-run average of 1.12. Since the advent of the lively ball in the nineteen-twenties, few pitchers have turned in yearly ERAs of under two runs per game. Yet, here was Gibson in 1968 establishing a one-season ERA that never had been matched, in or out of the lively

ball era, by any major league pitcher working a mini-
mum of 300 innings.

Bob's pitching efforts were duly noted by the expert
observers around the baseball world, who made the
Cardinals the favorites in the 1968 World Series against
the Detroit Tigers. The Tigers had a pitching hero of
their own in right-hander Denny McLain, who won
thirty-one games, the first time a major leaguer had
won as many as thirty since 1934. Still, Gibson, because of his experience under World Series stress, was
seen as St. Louis' edge over the Detroit club.

Bob never has allowed himself to become bogged
down by the weight of the clutch situations in which
he has so often been called upon. Late in the 1968
campaign, one veteran sportswriter remarked, "On days
when Gibson pitches, he'll tighten up to the point where
he might limit himself to twenty-eight laughs on the
way to the ballpark. On non-working days, the standard is thirty-five, at least."

Gibson always has laughed a lot, often at his own
comments which he delivers in a slightly high-pitched
voice. "He has a subtle, digging kind of sense of hum-
or," said former big leaguer Curt Flood, who was Bob's
roommate for seven seasons with the Cardinals. "He
likes to get anybody. If anybody can get anybody, he
can."

Bob explained his apparent lack of concern over
baseball in general, and his own pitching in particular,
this way: "No sense worrying about it away from the
park."

Once inside the park, Bob has been the epitome of
intense concentration on the task at hand. Such was
his demeanor at Busch Memorial Stadium in the early
afternoon of Wednesday, October 2, the opening day of
the 1968 World Series. The temperature hovered at

eighty degrees under brilliant sunshine, while a record St. Louis crowd of 54,692 fans took their seats.

There was no time for anything but concentration as Gibson prepared to take the mound against the Tigers for the first inning. The Detroit lineup was loaded with power. Willie Horton, who played leftfield, had hammered thirty-six home runs during the regular schedule; Norm Cash, the first baseman, and Bill Freehan, the catcher, each had twenty-five; and Jim Northrup, another outfielder, had twenty-one.

The Detroit favorite was Al Kaline, the all-time Tiger great who was appearing in his first World Series in his sixteen major league seasons. He no longer was a star, but Detroit club officials knew they had to find a spot for Kaline somewhere in the lineup, even if it meant breaking up the regular outfield alignment of Horton in left, Northrup in right and Mickey Stanley, a defensive ace, in center.

The Tigers solved their problem by moving Stanley to shortstop in place of weak-hitting Ray Oyler, and inserting Kaline in Northrup's regular rightfield spot, with Jim moving to center. While the move was chided in some circles as the ruination of the Detroit defense, there was no question that the substitution of Kaline's bat for Oyler's had to put teeth in the Tiger attack.

Just as Gibson was the obvious choice of St. Louis manager Red Schoendienst to pitch the first game of the Series for the Cardinals, Detroit boss Mayo Smith's choice of first-game pitcher was equally obvious. He sent his thirty-one-game winner, McLain, into combat against Gibson and the Cardinals. The Gibson-McLain matchup was billed as the confrontation of the century, the duel of the ages.

It lasted less than four innings. McLain, who seemed to be laboring throughout his stint, walked Cardinal rightfielder Roger Maris to open the bottom of the fourth. After Orlando Cepeda fouled out, catcher Tim McCarver also walked. Mike Shannon and Julian Javier followed with singles, and the Cards had three runs. After retiring St. Louis in the fifth with no further scoring against him, McLain was removed for a pinch hitter in the Tiger half of the sixth.

Meanwhile, Gibson was working strongly in the beautiful St. Louis sunshine. Bob struck out the leadoff batter, Dick McAuliffe, in the first inning. Stanley singled but was thrown out attempting to steal second. Then Kaline fanned for the third out. Gibson struck out three straight Tigers in the second, cutting down Cash, Horton and Northrup in effortless style. When Freehan struck out to open the Tiger third, Bob had struck out five straight batters. Don Wert broke the spell with a single to center, but Gibson allowed no further baserunners in the inning.

Following Stanley's single in their first turn at bat, the Tigers didn't get another hit off Gibson until the sixth, when McAuliffe singled and Kaline hit a double into the leftfield corner with two out. St. Louis led, 3-0, at that point and the tying run was at the plate. But Bob struck out Cash for the third out with a beautiful curveball.

Gibson paid credit to his catcher, McCarver, for helping him concentrate on retiring Cash. "After Kaline hit that double, Tim came to the mound," Bob recalled later. "I asked him who was up after Cash, and he said to forget who was next and get Cash. He was right. You worry about the guy up there swinging the bat, not somebody else who might be up some other time."

Known primarily as a fastball specialist, Bob also revealed an excellent curveball against the Tigers. Actually, he had been throwing curves with success for several seasons before the '68 Series. "I imagine the Tigers' scouting report must have said I threw mostly fastballs because they swung at breaking balls like they were surprised I could throw them," Bob remarked after the game.

He estimated that he threw the fastball seventy per cent of the time in the '68 Series opener, and also threw the slider twenty per cent and the curve ten per cent. "But most of my big strikeouts were on breaking pitches," Gibson pointed out. "Whenever I was behind I went to breaking pitches, because I was getting them over for strikes all day."

After six innings Bob had eleven strikeouts. The record for the most strikeouts in a single World Series game belonged to Sandy Koufax, who had whiffed fifteen Yankees in the opening game of the 1963 Series.

It seemed that every last fan in the biggest crowd ever to see a major league ballgame in St. Louis knew that Gibson was drawing close to a strikeout mark. As the Tigers continued to strike out, a group of standees back of home plate shouted encouragement to Bob. Every time Gibson threw another strike the crowd cheered. If Bob retired a Detroit batter by some means other than a strikeout, the crowd moaned, as they did when Horton opened the Tiger seventh by lining out to Dal Maxvill at shortstop. But Gibson ran his strikeout total to thirteen by fanning Northrup and Freehan to end the inning.

In the bottom of the seventh, Lou Brock, the Cards' whirling dervish of a centerfielder, gave St. Louis its fourth run when he lined a homer into the right-center bleachers off relief pitcher Pat Dobson. But by this time the only thing that mattered to the St. Louis fans was Gibson's quest for a strikeout record.

It seemed Bob would reach his goal with ease when he fanned the first man to face him in the eighth. It was Ed Mathews, one of the greatest sluggers in National League history with the Braves, now closing out his career with the Tigers. Gibson sent Mathews back to the dugout with great dispatch. Now he needed only one more victim to tie Koufax's record.

He didn't get his man in the eighth. Gates Brown, batting for Dobson, flied out to Brock, and so did McAuliffe.

In the top of the ninth inning there was near pandemonium in the stands of Busch Memorial Stadium. A victory by the home team long had been assured, but the fans now pleaded for more Gibson strikeouts. The Tigers, fighting valiantly to the end, got their fifth hit of the game when Stanley led off the inning with a single to center. With the heart of Detroit's batting order—Kaline, Cash and Horton—due up, the Tigers still had to be given a chance to get back into the game.

Gibson didn't give them the chance. He tied Koufax's record by striking out Kaline on a one-two pitch. It was the third time Kaline had gone down on strikes, though he also had delivered Detroit's only extra-base blow of the day, that sixth-inning double.

Cash went down easier. Bob poured a fastball past the Tiger first baseman for his record-breaking sixteenth strikeout. Then, for good measure, he also whiffed Horton as the crowd virtually exploded. Fans, policemen, ushers, everybody jumped up screaming in an ovation for the Cardinal record-breaker. It later was estimated that the grateful St. Louis fans had given Bob the longest standing ovation in the city's long and proud baseball history.

It was a perfect ending to a perfect day for baseball.

Wednesday, October 2, 1968, at St. Louis

Detroit (A)	AB.	R.	H.
McAuliffe, 2b	4	0	1
Stanley, ss	4	0	2
Kaline, rf	4	0	1
Cash, 1b	4	0	0
Horton, lf	4	0	0
Northrup, cf	3	0	0
Freehan, c	2	0	0
Wert, 3b	2	0	1
bMathews	1	0	0
Tracewski, 3b	0	0	0
McLain, p	1	0	0
aMatchick	1	0	0
Dobson, p	0	0	0
cBrown	1	0	0
McMahon, p	0	0	0
Totals	31	0	5

St. Louis (N)	AB.	R.	H.
Brock, lf	4	1	1
Flood, cf	4	0	1
Maris, rf	3	1	0
Cepeda, 1b	4	0	0
McCarver, c	3	1	1
Shannon, 3b	4	1	2
Javier, 2b	3	0	1
Maxvill, ss	2	0	0
GIBSON, p	2	0	0
Totals	29	4	6

```
Detroit ............................. 0 0 0   0 0 0   0 0 0—0
St. Louis ........................... 0 0 0   3 0 0   1 0 x—4
```

Detroit	IP.	H.	R.	ER.	HR.	SO.	BB.
McLain (Loser)	5	3	3	2	0	3	3
Dobson	2	2	1	1	0	1	1
McMahon	1	1	0	0	0	0	0

St. Louis	IP.	H.	R.	ER.	HR.	SO.	BB.
Gibson (Winner)	9	5	0	0	0	17	1

aGrounded out for McLain in sixth. bStruck out for Wert in eighth. cFlied out for Dobson in eighth. Runs batted in—Brock, Shannon, Javier 2. Two-base hit—Kaline. Three-base hit—McCarver. Home run—Brock. Stolen bases—Brock, Javier, Flood. Sacrifice hit—Gibson. Left on bases—Detroit 5, St. Louis 6. Bases on balls—Off McLain 3 (Maxvill, Maris, McCarver), off Dobson 1 (Javier), off Gibson 1 (Freehan). Struck out—By McLain 3 (Shannon, Javier, Gibson), by Gibson 17 (McAuliffe, Kaline 3, Cash 3, Horton 2, Northrup 2, Freehan 2, McLain, Wert, Stanley, Mathews). Umpires—Gorman (NL), at plate; Honochick (AL), first base; Landes (NL), second base; Kinnamon (AL), third base; Harvey (NL), left field line; Haller (AL), right field line. Time of game—2:29. Attendance—54,692.

The Mets' Miracle

On the morning of July 17, 1969, two American astronauts, Neil Armstrong and Buzz Aldrin, were en route to becoming the first men to walk on the surface of the moon.

On the same morning, the New York Mets awoke to find themselves firmly established as pennant contenders in the National League, following the conclusion of the most critical nine-day period of their existence.

It will be left to historians to decide which of the two above events was the most miraculous. The feeling is that the journey of approximately 200,000 miles negotiated by the two astronauts wasn't quite as far as the climb to prominence of the Mets, who had been buried in the nether regions of sport for seven years.

The Mets, known as the "Amazins," a label affixed on them by their first and most popular manager, Casey Stengel, had just completed their second series victory in two weeks over the Chicago Cubs at about the time Armstrong and Aldrin started out on their trip to find rocks. The Mets had stopped the front-running Cubs, seemingly headed for their first pennant in nearly a quarter-century behind the fiery leadership of manager Leo Durocher, in two of three contests at their Shea Stadium home in Queens, New York. Now the Mets had won two of three games from the Cubs at the latter's home in Wrigley Field, Chicago. They had done it convincingly too, polishing off the Chicagoans in the finale of the three-game set, 9-5.

For a team with a seven-year history of futility unmatched in all the years of baseball, this was very heady stuff. The Mets became the darlings of the sports world because of their unrivaled record for the kind of ineptness that inspires sympathy. They had lost one hundred and twenty games, a record for a single year, in their first season of 1962. In seven years they had lost a total of seven hundred and thirty-seven games, more than one hundred and five per year. Only once had they finished higher than tenth and last place in the National League: in 1968, the first year under manager Gil Hodges, they finished ninth with seventy-three victories against eighty-nine defeats. Their team batting average of .228 was appallingly low.

The National League added two new teams in 1969 —the Montreal Expos and San Diego Padres. Then the League divided its twelve teams into separate Eastern and Western divisions with six teams in each. The Mets, of course, were placed in the Eastern grouping and immediately were consigned to sixth place for the first year of divisional play. This was essentially the same squad that finished the 1968 season. There had been no major offseason trades. People knew that Tom Seaver, a right-hander, and Jerry Koosman, a left-hander, had the potential to become outstanding pitchers, and that outfielder Cleon Jones appeared to be a good hitter.

But the Mets seemed to have little else to offer, and selecting them for last place in the East seemed a safe choice to most baseball observers at the beginning of the '69 campaign.

The Mets were surprisingly effective—for them— during the first two months of the season. They won nine and lost eleven in April, and were even with twelve victories and twelve defeats in May.

In June, Hodges had his Mets winging. Beginning with seven consecutive victories over the National

League's west coast clubs, San Francisco, Los Angeles and San Diego, the Mets stormed to nineteen victories in twenty-eight starts for the month. It was, by far, the most successful month in club history to that time. After three months of play in '69, the Mets had won forty games. In 1962, their first season of play, the Mets won a total of forty games.

There seemed little doubt, even among the most cynical observers, that the Mets would escape the cellar this season. Pennant contention? Out of the question. But a respectable finish among the top four teams of the six-team division now seemed quite likely.

Despite their strong showing against the Chicago Cubs through the middle of July, the Mets closed badly that month. After completing their second three-game series of the month with Chicago, the Mets trailed the first-place Chicago team by three and one-half games, and were resting comfortably in second place, six games ahead of third-place St. Louis.

But in the last two weeks of July, the Mets lost seven games, including three in a row to arch-nemesis Houston. When the National League grew from eight to ten teams in 1962, Houston and New York were the two new clubs. Since that time, the Astros had succeeded in defeating the Mets nearly every time the clubs met.

When July ended, the Mets were six games behind the Cubs and their hold on second place was tenuous. Their place in the pennant race seemed to be lost and reality apparently was taking over.

In the month of August, New York was scheduled to face the strong teams from the National League's West Division, the Atlanta Braves, the Cincinnati Reds and the west coast teams. It looked like reality would soon show its stark side. For the first thirteen days of the month that's what happened. In that span the Mets played fourteen games, winning seven and losing seven. Three more losses were to the Houston Astros, who were going nowhere in their Western race but still seemed to have a hex on the New Yorkers.

Now the Cubs' margin over the Mets was a whopping nine and one-half games and the date was August 14. From a similar date and from even further back, the Miracle Giants had battled back to capture the 1951 National League pennant in a playoff with the Brooklyn Dodgers. But any comparison between the 1951 Giants—the Giants of Willie Mays and Monte Irvin and Sal Maglie and Alvin Dark and Don Mueller and Eddie Stanky—and the Mets of 1969 seemed laughable.

The Mets, it seemed, had gone about as far as they could go. The Cubs were rushing to clinch the pennant. The Mets would have to be wary of the oncoming Cardinals and Pirates in order to hold on to their second-place position. There weren't many willing to bet the Mets would keep from falling all the way to fourth place.

Suddenly, unaccountably, the Mets righted themselves again. Starting with two doubleheader sweeps in two days against San Diego, New York reeled off twelve victories in its next thirteen games. They swept three straight at home from the Los Angeles Dodgers and won two of three from the San Francisco Giants. For the last two weeks of August the Mets won fourteen and lost only three, and on the morning of September 1, the supposedly beaten Mets were only four games out of first place.

As amazing as the Mets had been in August—twenty-one wins, ten losses, their best month ever—they were truly colossal in September. They roared to victory after victory, while Chicago went into a dreadful tailspin. Starting with a 3-0 shutout over the Philadelphia Phillies by right-hander Don Cardwell, on September 6, the Mets embarked on a ten-game winning streak, including two wins over the staggering Cubs and three wins over Pittsburgh.

Day after day, the Mets won, facing the pennant pressure they were experiencing for the first time with equanimity and rare poise. The Cubs, who were supposed to be the poised veterans, the ones who wouldn't fold, were falling apart. Between September 3-11, Chicago lost eight straight starts.

The culmination of the Mets' winning skein and the Cubs' run of defeats came in a night doubleheader at Shea Stadium against the Montreal Expos on September 10. The Mets won both games and went into first place for the first time in their history. What had started out as an impossible dream and a totally preposterous notion suddenly was becoming possible and plausible.

For two more weeks the Mets won and the Cubs lost. Finally, on the night of September 24, before 56,586 screaming Met loyalists, Gary Gentry, a rookie right-hander, spun a four-hit 6-0 victory over the Cardinals. The victory gave the Mets the division title and pandemonium broke loose in Shea Stadium. The Mets celebrated by breaking open fifteen cases of champagne and spilling them over each other. Hardly a drop of the bubbly passed through the lips of the youthful Mets, many of whom looked too young to drink anyway.

That the Mets were destined to win the Eastern Division title all along was made clear in several ways in September. The Mets again broke their team record for one month by fashioning a brilliant 23-7 won-lost mark. This gave them forty-four wins and seventeen defeats over the last two months of the season, and a 37-10 record from the middle of August to the end of the season. Even when the Mets lost, it was done sublimely. Bob Moose of Pittsburgh no-hitted them on September 20. The most improbable victory was a 4-3 triumph over the Cardinals on September 15, in which St. Louis southpaw Steve Carlton established a one-game mark by striking out nineteen batters. A hustling young outfielder named Ron Swoboda clouted a pair of two-run homers off Carlton to enable the Mets to overcome all those strikeouts.

The Mets' divisional title was the talk of New York. Even the rival Yankees, based in the Bronx and losing money and fans while the Mets prospered to the tune of more than two million paying customers, were caught up in Metmania. The president of the Yankees sent a telegram to M. Donald Grant, the Mets' chairman of the board, which read this way:

"Congratulations on being Number One. Am rooting for you to hang in there and take all the marbles. As a New Yorker I am ecstatic, as a baseball person I am immensely pleased and as a Yankee I consider suicide the easy option. Signed, Michael Burke, New York Yankees Inc."

Because of the newly aligned divisions in the major leagues in 1969, the Mets still were not in the World Series. They had to meet the Atlanta Braves, champions of the Western Division, in a championship playoff series, the winner of which would then qualify to play for the world title.

The Braves, like the Mets, were surprise winners of their division, though their upset triumph paled by comparison to that of the Mets. During the regular season Atlanta won ninety-three games and lost sixty-nine, a full seven games off the pace of New York, which won one hundred and lost sixty-two. But the Braves boasted one of the strongest batting orders in the major leagues, led by Hammerin' Henry Aaron, Orlando Cepeda and Rico Carty. Practically every member of the Atlanta starting lineup could belt baseballs over buildings at any given time. The Mets' pitching, second best in the league (behind St. Louis) during the regular season, was in for a severe test.

Compounding the problem was the fact that the first two games of the best-of-five series were scheduled for Atlanta, where the Braves' sluggers were particularly devastating. Could the Amazing Mets continue their amazing ways?

They could indeed, but not in the manner that would have been expected. The series figured to be a battle between Atlanta's hitting and New York's pitching. It turned out to be a battle between Atlanta's hitting—and New York's even better hitting. The Mets swept three straight games, two in Atlanta, the third in New York, and the scores indicate how the Mets suddenly turned killers at bat—9-5, 11-6, and 7-4.

The Mets started their big three pitchers, Seaver, Koosman and Gentry, in the three games, and one of them was a winner. Seaver, a twenty-five-game winner in the regular season, making him the most successful pitcher in the big leagues for '69, was removed for a pinch hitter in the eighth inning of the first game in Atlanta. In that inning, the Mets, who had been trailing, 5-4, exploded for five runs to win the game.

The 11-6 slugfest in the second game began as a rout by the Mets. They raced to an 8-0 lead inside of four innings, routing Braves' starter Ron Reed. But Koosman couldn't stand prosperity, and was knocked from the mound when Atlanta scored five times in the bottom of the sixth to reduce the Mets' margin to 9-6. Aaron, who blasted a home run in each game of the series, was leading an Atlanta charge that promised to take the Braves to a come-from-behind victory.

But New York received shutout pitching from its

late-inning relief pitchers, and Cleon Jones hit a two-run homer in the seventh to close out the scoring.

On October 6, the two teams squared off in Shea Stadium before 53,195 delirious New York devotees. This time the Braves broke on top with two runs in the first inning. In the third, Atlanta put runners on second and third with nobody out and Hodges removed his starter, Gentry, in favor of fireballer Nolan Ryan, whose wildness was his best-known characteristic.

Ryan escaped the third with no Atlanta scoring and pitched the remainder of the game. He walked only two men, and made only one bad pitch. Orlando Cepeda cuffed it for a two-run home run in the fifth inning.

Meanwhile centerfielder Tommie Agee and second baseman Ken Boswell hit Met homers for the second consecutive day, and were joined in the longball derby by third baseman Wayne Garrett, who hadn't hit a homer since the previous May 6. With three runs in the fifth and one more in the sixth, New York had all it needed to close out the game and the playoff series.

Only a few minutes after the Mets had disposed of the Braves, the Baltimore Orioles completed a three-game sweep of the Minnesota Twins in the American League championship playoffs.

If ever a team were guaranteed to frighten an inexperienced young team like the Mets, it was the 1969 Baltimore Orioles. They won one hundred nine games during the regular season, competing in the only major league division that didn't have an expansion team. This was a team with experience, with a multitude of skills, with character. In 1966, they had swept the World Series in four straight games from the Los Angeles Dodgers, despite the presence of Sandy Koufax and Don Drysdale in the Dodger pitching rotation. Injuries had halted the Orioles in 1967 and 1968. But they were healthy now, this team of Frank Robinson in right, Brooks Robinson at third, Boog Powell at first, and a host of other stars. Baltimore, many people close to the team averred, was the best team to represent the American League in the World Series since the Yankee juggernaut of years before.

Against such a team, the Mets figured to be reduced to rubble. Many people, sentimentalists no doubt, were calling the Mets "a team of destiny." But to most realistic appraisers of the situation, the only destiny that awaited the Mets was annihilation by the Orioles.

And when Mike Cuellar outpitched Seaver in the first game of the Series at Baltimore, and Baltimore won, 4-1, reality at last seemed to have triumphed. Don Buford, the Orioles' leftfielder, led off against Seaver with a home run, and Baltimore coasted from there.

The Mets scored their only run in the seventh after Baltimore already had scored all four of its runs. The New York run came home on a sacrifice fly by light-hitting second baseman Al Weis, after the Mets had loaded the bases with none out. But the left-handed Cuellar pitched out of that jam and ended up with a six-hitter.

More than ever, the Orioles now were hailed as one of baseball's greatest powerhouse teams, certainly one of the greatest teams in all of sports history. The Orioles, for their part, cultivated an air of superiority. Before the Series even had begun, Frank Robinson, the Baltimore leader, had joked about the Mets and the relatively small threat they seemed to represent.

One of New York's lesser players was a pinch runner and substitute outfielder named Rod Gaspar. During the Orioles' pennant-clinching ceremony, Robinson had derisively shouted, "Bring on Ron Gaspar!"

"That's Rod, stupid," corrected Merv Rettenmund, another Oriole outfielder.

"Okay, bring on Rod Stupid," finished Robinson.

After the first game of the Series, the joke was on the Orioles. In the second game, a duel between left-handers Jerry Koosman and Dave McNally, the Mets won out, 2-1, when Ed Charles, Jerry Grote and Al Weis hit consecutive ninth-inning singles after two were out. Donn Clendenon, a slugging first baseman acquired by the Mets in midseason, belted a homer in the fourth inning for New York's other run as Koosman limited the powerful Orioles to two hits, both singles in the seventh inning, when Baltimore scored its lone run.

In the third game, first of the Series played in New York, more Met magic took place. Gary Gentry, who pitched into the seventh, and Nolan Ryan held Baltimore's batters to four hits. The Mets made only six hits themselves, but two were for the distance. Tommie Agee led off the New York first with a homer, and Ed Kranepool hit one in the eighth for the final Mets' run in a 5-0 victory.

In addition to his home run, Agee was the fielding hero for the Mets. He made two sensational catches in centerfield, personally preventing five Baltimore runs. In the fourth inning he went to the base of the wall and made a back-handed catch of a towering smash by Ellie Hendricks with two men on base. In the seventh inning, with the bases loaded, Paul Blair of the Orioles smacked a tremendous drive to right-center. Agee, playing over towards left, raced across the field at full speed and made a sliding one-handed catch while falling to the grass.

With plays like those of Agee, momentum now seemed to belong to the Mets. The fourth game was a rematch between Seaver and Cuellar, and both men pitched brilliantly. Clendenon homered for one New York run in the second inning. The run held up until the Baltimore ninth when Frank Robinson scored on a sacrifice fly by Brooks Robinson. By all rights, the ball hit by Brooks should have been a triple. But Swoboda, never known for his defensive work, continued New York's sensational outfielding with a diving, one-handed grab of Robinson's sinking flyball.

The Mets scored the run that gave them a 2-1 victory in the bottom of the tenth. It scored in the person of Rod Gaspar, the man the Orioles had found so funny a few days before. Gaspar was running for Grote, who led off the inning with a double. When J. C. Martin, batting for Seaver, attempted to sacrifice Gaspar to third base, the ball was fielded by Oriole relief pitcher Pete Richert, whose throw toward first struck Martin on the left wrist. As the ball rolled into the outfield, Gaspar crossed the plate with the winning run.

The fifth game, played October 16 at Shea Stadium, drew 57,397 zealots, each hoping against hope that the Mets could sweep the three Series games in New York and close out the fall classic in five games overall. The odds, though, favored a second Baltimore victory, which would send the Series back to the Orioles' home field two days later.

Baltimore had every intention of returning the Series to the friendlier confines of its home field. Against Koosman, who had limited them to two hits in the second game, the Orioles teed off for three runs in the third inning. Two runs scored on a homer by Frank Robinson, who had made only two hits in the previous four games.

McNally, the losing pitcher to Koosman in game two of the Series, was flawless until the sixth. Then he hit Cleon Jones with a pitch and Clendenon unloaded his third homer of the Series into the leftfield stands, no easy feat for a left-handed batter.

Al Weis led off the Mets' seventh against McNally.

Weis was this type of hitter. In two hundred and forty-seven official plate appearances during the 1969 regular season, he batted a minuscule .215 and hit two home runs. He promptly tagged McNally's second pitch into the leftfield stands to tie the score. If ever there was a time to believe in miracles, the time was now.

Even the Orioles were quickly becoming believers. When the Mets had started out in the baseball business in 1962, Casey Stengel once had asked his collection of diamond misfits, "Can't anybody here play this game?" Now the Orioles were asking another question of the Mets: "When are you going to stop this madness already and leave us alone?"

The Orioles' anguish nearly was over, and, true to the form of this Series, Baltimore's players hastened their demise by making two errors on the same play.

With Eddie Watt pitching in relief for the Orioles, Cleon Jones doubled to lead off New York's half of the eighth inning. One out later, Swoboda also doubled, scoring Jones. When Grote grounded to Powell at first base, the ball was fumbled, and when Watt tried to make a late play on Grote, the pitcher fumbled Powell's throw toward the bag. Swoboda scored all the way from second on the double error.

That did it. In the ninth, Koosman walked Frank Robinson but Powell forced him at second base. Brooks Robinson flied out to Swoboda.

Dave Johnson, the Orioles' second baseman was the last out. He hit Koosman's pitch well, on a line to leftfield. Cleon Jones lined up the catch and when the ball landed in his glove, it was as if all of New York City had turned upside down. Fans poured onto the field from every direction, and rather than stop them from racing across the field to pummel their Met heroes, the special policemen who were working the security detail at Shea Stadium raced right alongside the fans. Policemen are baseball fans, too. Indeed, in that season of 1969, everyone seemed to be a Met fan, including God. How else to explain such a miracle?

Even Jones, immediately upon recording the last out of the incredible World Series victory over the Orioles, acknowledged the intervention of a Divine Being. With the ball tucked safely in his glove, Jones dropped to one knee before rising to run off the field.

Why the genuflection? "Someone was good to us," Jones explained later.

Fifth and Final Game of 1969 World Series

Baltimore (A.L.)   **New York (N.L.)**

Thursday, October 16, 1969, At Shea Stadium, New York

	AB.	R.	H.		AB.	R.	H.
Buford, lf	4	0	0	Agee, cf	3	0	1
Blair, cf	4	0	0	Harrelson, ss	4	0	0
F. Robinson, rf	3	1	1	Jones, lf	3	2	1
Powell, 1b	4	0	1	Clendenon, 1b	3	1	1
†Salmon	0	0	0	Swoboda, rf	4	1	2
B. Robinson, 3b	4	0	0	Charles, 3b	4	0	0
Johnson, 2b	4	0	1	Grote, c	4	0	0
Etchebarren, c	3	0	0	Weis, 2b	4	1	1
Belanger, ss	3	1	1	Koosman, p	3	0	1
McNally, p	2	1	1		—	—	—
*Motton	1	0	0	Totals	32	5	7
Watt, p	0	0	0				
	—	—	—				
Totals	32	3	5				

```
Baltimore ............... 0 0 3  0 0 0  0 0 0—3
New York ............... 0 0 0  0 0 2  1 2 x—5
```

*Grounded out for McNally in eighth. †Ran for Powell in ninth. Error—Powell, Watt. Runs batted in—McNally 2, F. Robinson, Clendenon 2, Weis, Swoboda. Two-base hits—Koosman, Jones, Swoboda. Home runs—McNally, F. Robinson, Clendenon, Weis. Stolen base—Agee. Left on bases—Baltimore 3, New York 6. Earned runs—Baltimore 3, New York 4. Bases on balls—Off McNally 2, off Koosman 1. Struck out—By McNally 6, by Watt 1, by Koosman 5. Pitching records—Off McNally 5 hits and 3 runs in 7 innings; off Watt 2 hits and 2 runs in 1 inning. Hit by pitcher—By McNally (Jones). Winning pitcher—Koosman. Losing pitcher—Watt. Umpires—DiMuro (A. L.), Weyer (N. L.), Soar (A. L.), Secory (N. L.), Napp (A. L.), Crawford (N. L.). Time—2:14. Attendance—57,397.

NEW YORK METS' 1969 WORLD SERIES BATTING AVERAGES

Player-Position	G.	AB.	R.	H.	2B.	3B.	HR	R.B.I.	B.A.
Weis, 2b	5	11	1	5	0	0	1	3	.455
Swoboda, rf	4	15	1	6	1	0	0	1	.400
Clendenon, 1b	4	14	4	5	1	0	3	4	.357
Boswell, 2b	1	3	1	1	0	0	0	0	.333
Gentry, p	1	3	0	1	1	0	0	2	.333
Kranepool, 1b	1	4	1	1	0	0	1	1	.250
Grote, c	5	19	1	4	2	0	0	1	.211
Harrelson, ss	5	17	1	3	0	0	0	0	.176
Agee, cf	5	18	1	3	0	0	1	1	.167
Jones, lf	5	19	2	3	1	0	0	0	.158
Koosman, p	2	7	0	1	1	0	0	0	.143
Charles, 3b	4	15	1	2	1	0	0	0	.133
Shamsky, ph-rf	3	6	0	0	0	0	0	0	.000
Seaver, p.	2	4	0	0	0	0	0	0	.000
Gaspar, ph-rf-pr	3	2	1	0	0	0	0	0	.000
Garrett, 3b	2	1	0	0	0	0	0	0	.000
Dyer, ph	1	1	0	0	0	0	0	0	.000
Taylor, p	2	0	0	0	0	0	0	0	.000
Cardwell, p	1	0	0	0	0	0	0	0	.000
Martin, ph	1	0	0	0	0	0	0	0	.000
Ryan, p	1	0	0	0	0	0	0	0	.000
Totals	5	159	15	35	8	0	6	13	.220

Dyer grounded out for Seaver in sixth inning of first game.

Gaspar grounded out for Cardwell in seventh inning of first game and ran and scored for Grote in tenth inning of first game.

Shamsky grounded out for Taylor in ninth inning of first game and grounded out for Charles in ninth inning of fourth game.

Martin sacrificed and was safe on error for Seaver in tenth inning of fourth game.

BALTIMORE ORIOLES' 1969 WORLD SERIES BATTING AVERAGES

Player-Position	G.	AB.	R.	H.	2B.	3B.	HR	R.B.I.	B.A.
Dalrymple, ph	2	2	0	2	0	0	0	0	1.000
Cuellar, p	2	5	0	2	0	0	0	1	.400
Powell, 1b	5	19	0	5	0	0	0	0	.263
Belanger, ss	5	15	2	3	0	0	0	1	.200
McNally, p	2	5	1	1	0	0	1	2	.200
F. Robinson, rf	5	16	2	3	0	0	1	1	.188
Blair, cf	5	20	1	2	0	0	0	0	.100
Buford, lf	5	20	1	2	1	0	1	2	.100
Hendricks, c	3	10	1	1	0	0	0	0	.100
Johnson, 2b	5	16	1	1	0	0	0	0	.063
B. Robinson, 3b	5	19	0	1	0	0	0	2	.053
Etchebarren, c	2	6	0	0	0	0	0	0	.000
Palmer, p	1	2	0	0	0	0	0	0	.000
May, ph	2	1	0	0	0	0	0	0	.000
Motton, ph	1	1	0	0	0	0	0	0	.000
Salmon, pr	2	0	0	0	0	0	0	0	.000
Watt, p	2	0	0	0	0	0	0	0	.000
Hall, p	1	0	0	0	0	0	0	0	.000
Leonhard, p	1	0	0	0	0	0	0	0	.000
Rettenmund, pr	1	0	0	0	0	0	0	0	.000
Richert, p	1	0	0	0	0	0	0	0	.000
Totals	5	157	9	23	1	0	3	9	.146

Rettenmund ran for F. Robinson in ninth inning of second game.

May walked for Palmer in seventh inning of third game and struck out for Cuellar in eighth inning of fourth game.

Dalrymple singled for Leonhard in ninth inning of third game and singled for Watt in tenth inning of fourth game.

Salmon ran for Dalrymple in ninth inning of third game and ran for Powell in ninth inning of fifth game.

Motton grounded out for McNally in eighth inning of fifth game.

NEW YORK METS' 1969 WORLD SERIES PITCHING RECORDS

Pitcher	G.	GS.	CG.	IP.	H.	R.	ER.	HR.	SO.	BB.	W.	L.	Pct.	ERA.
Gentry	1	1	0	6 2/3	3	0	0	0	4	5	1	0	1.000	0.00
Taylor	2	0	0	2 1/3	0	0	0	0	3	1	0	0	.000	0.00
Ryan	1	0	0	2 1/3	1	0	0	0	3	2	0	0	.000	0.00
Cardwell	1	0	0	1	0	0	0	0	0	0	0	0	.000	0.00
Koosman	2	2	1	17 2/3	7	4	4	2	9	4	2	0	1.000	2.04
Seaver	2	2	1	15	12	5	5	1	9	3	1	1	.500	3.00
Totals	5	5	2	45	23	9	9	3	28	15	4	1	.800	1.80

Saves—Taylor, Ryan.

BALTIMORE ORIOLES' 1969 WORLD SERIES PITCHING RECORDS

Pitcher	G.	GS.	CG.	IP.	H.	R.	ER.	HR.	SO.	BB.	W.	L.	Pct.	ERA.
Cuellar	2	2	1	16	13	2	2	1	13	4	1	0	1.000	1.13
McNally	2	2	1	16	11	5	5	3	13	5	0	1	.000	2.81
Watt	2	0	0	3	4	2	1	0	3	0	0	1	.000	3.00
Leonhard	1	0	0	2	1	1	1	1	1	1	0	0	.000	4.50
Palmer	1	1	0	6	5	4	4	1	5	4	0	1	.000	6.00
Hall	1	0	0	0*	1	1	0	0	0	1	0	1	.000	0.00
Richert	1	0	0	0†	0	0	0	0	0	0	0	0	.000	0.00
Totals	5	5	2	43	35	15	13	6	35	15	1	4	.200	2.72

*Pitched to two batters in tenth inning of fourth game.
†Pitched to one batter in tenth inning of fourth game.

Hank Aaron Pursues the Babe

The first name in *The Baseball Encyclopedia,* a compendium of information on every player who has appeared in the major leagues, is that of Henry Louis Aaron. The reason is simple. The two "a's" at the beginning of his last name place him first in the alphabetical listing of players.

As 1973 approached, Henry Aaron was closing in on becoming the first name on another baseball list. With six hundred and seventy-three career home runs before 1973, Hammerin' Hank was threatening to eclipse the record most baseball historians had sworn never could be broken—Babe Ruth's magic seven hundred and fourteen lifetime circuits.

Going into his nineteenth big league season, the Atlanta Braves' star already had gained a top rung in two of baseball's most cherished categories. In 1972, though he suffered the pains of an arthritic neck, Hank became the all-time major league career record-holder in total bases, and the National League king in runs batted in.

With two hundred and thirty-one total bases in 1972, Aaron pushed his career figure to six thousand, one hundred, and seventy-two. Stan Musial, the Hall of Fame immortal of the St. Louis Cardinals, had six thousand, one hundred and thirty-four total bases during his brilliant career, which included three thousand, six hundred and thirty hits, an all-time National League mark. Hank surpassed "Stan the Man" in total bases even though he still trailed far behind the Cardinal great in hits with three thousand, three hundred and ninety-one. This indicated that Hank was a far more productive longball producer than even Musial had been, or for that matter, than anyone else who had preceded Aaron into the big leagues.

Henry Aaron was born in Mobile, Alabama, on February 5, 1934. His father, a laborer, had eight children to support. "But we owned our own home," recalls Hank. "We helped our father build it. We didn't have any new lumber, but we took pieces of old lumber out of houses that had been torn down nearby."

Aaron played high school baseball and football in Mobile, but preferred baseball. After his graduation he signed to play with the Indianapolis Clowns of the Negro American League. It was 1951, and though Jackie Robinson had broken baseball's color barrier four years before, there still was not wholehearted acceptance of blacks in the major leagues. Aaron chose to play in the Negro League, rather than attempt to play with an established integrated team.

He was an infielder then, a shortstop mostly. Hank was so outstanding with the Clowns that the Braves, then based in Boston, acquired his contract and assigned him to their Northern League farm team in Eau Claire, Wisconsin. Aaron batted .336 for the Eau Claire team in 1952. From there it was on to Jacksonville with the Sally League in 1953 and, finally, promotion to the Braves, by then located in Milwaukee, for the 1954 campaign. Hank was twenty years old.

He made a good, though tentative, showing as a rookie with the Braves in 1954, batting .280 and connecting for thirteen home runs. The first came on April 23, off Vic Raschi, a curve balling right-hander who had been a star for many years with the New York Yankees, but now was winding up his career with the St. Louis Cardinals.

By his third season in the National League, 1956,

Aaron was the league's batting champion, with a .328 average. It was his first of two batting titles. He was to lead the NL again in 1959 with a .355 mark, his one-season high.

But Hank didn't win only batting championships. Four times he led the National League in home runs, and an equal number of times he was the senior circuit's runs-batted-in titlist. Along the way to immortality, he achieved some immense major league records: most years, 100 or more runs scored: fifteen; most consecutive years with twenty or more home runs: eighteen; most years leading the league in total bases: eight.

When Roger Maris broke Babe Ruth's single-season home run mark with his sixty-one blasts in 1961, Aaron was one of baseball's supreme sluggers. "I remember everyone saying, 'Well, okay, somebody broke Ruth's record for one year,'" Hank recalls. "But they all felt that there was no way Babe's seven hundred and fourteen could be reached. I think it was then that I first became aware of that record. I never paid attention to things like that before."

Hank always seemed unaware of his records at any particular moment in time. Asked by a reporter one day what his batting average was, he replied, "Anybody with a pencil can figure out batting averages. You do the figuring and I'll do the hitting."

An unorthodox batsman, Hank didn't realize when he came to the major leagues that a ballplayer doesn't hold his bat with the label facing the pitcher. Once this was pointed out to him. But Aaron shrugged and said, "I get paid for hitting, not for reading."

Consistency has been Aaron's trademark throughout his fabulous career. He never has hit as many as fifty homers in a season, a feat managed four times by Babe Ruth, and twice by Willie Mays, who for a long time seemed the logical challenger for Ruth's all-time homer mark. But, through 1972, Hank had belted homers in the thirties or forties a total of fourteen times, a figure that topped all other players, even Babe himself. Hank was second in all-time RBIs to Babe's 2,209. Aaron smashed a three-run homer during an Atlanta 13-9 victory over Houston on July 3, 1972, to become the first National Leaguer over 2,000 RBIs. By the completion of 1972, Aaron had pushed his RBI total to 2,037.

When Hank belted a homer off Pittsburgh's Nellie Briles in an 8-3 losing cause on July 19, 1972, he tied one of Ruth's foremost slugging accomplishments. The blow was Aaron's 659th as a member of the Braves, equaling Babe's mark for homers with one team. Ruth hit 659 of his total of 714 while playing for the Yankees.

Actually, the symbolic homer in Hank's quest of Ruth's record was his six hundredth. "When I reached six hundred, it suddenly dawned on me that I could make seven hundred," Aaron said. "I hadn't thought too much about even getting to six hundred, but when I did, that gave me the idea that I would play a few more seasons."

Perhaps that explains Hank's fantastic longball explosion throughout the 1971 season. Though he was nursing aches and pains and had to be moved to first base on many occasions because outfielding was becoming too strenuous for his thirty-seven-year-old legs, Aaron belted forty-seven roundtrippers in 1971, more than he had managed ever before in one year. It wasn't good enough to lead the league. That honor fell to Pittsburgh's Willie Stargell, who busted forty-eight baseballs into the stands. But Hank's forty-seven homers represented an amazing achievement for a man of his years.

The six-hundredth homer on the Aaron ledger came on a Tuesday night early in the 1971 season, April 27. Henry already had hit seven homers in April, one of his fastest starts. Five nights earlier, he had hit his 599th homer off San Diego's Dave Roberts.

Many players drawing close to a major milestone tend to become rattled and begin to press to reach the magic mark. Willie Mays didn't hit his 600th homer until a couple of weeks after his 599th.

Before arriving at Atlanta Stadium to face the San Francisco Giants this particular night, Hank read what Gaylord Perry, the strong-armed right-hander scheduled to pitch for the west coast team, had said about him: "If Aaron hits his 600th home run against me, he's going to have to earn it."

In the third inning, with leftfielder Ralph Garr on base and the Braves trailing, 3-2, Henry hit one of Perry's fastballs 350 feet over the leftfield fence. As the ball disappeared over the wall, Mays, playing centerfield for the Giants, stood watching with his hands on his hips. When the inning was over Mays trotted into his dugout but paused en route to slap Aaron on the back as Hank moved out to take his place in rightfield.

The game eventually went into extra innings, and Mays, some of his thunder stolen by Aaron's historic homer, delivered the game-winning hit in the top of the tenth. The Giants won the contest, 6-5. But all the post-game conversation dealt with Hank's third-inning homer.

"I knew all along I'd hit it off a pitcher I knew," Aaron said. "I guessed fastball and that's what I got. Perry tried to jam me, but he missed by about two inches and I got a clean shot at it. I knew it was gone the minute I hit it."

Then, reflectively, summing up his entire philosophy on hitting as he looked forward to more homers and more records, Aaron added, "When I go up to the plate I've got a bat in my hands and all the pitcher has is a ball. I figure that makes it all in my favor."

Hank Aaron's Sixth Hundredth Home Run
Tuesday, April 27, 1971, at Atlanta

San Francisco	AB.	R.	H.	Atlanta	AB.	R.	H.
Bonds, rf	5	1	2	Jackson, cf	5	0	1
Foster, rf	1	0	0	Garr, lf	5	2	4
Speier, ss	6	2	3	AARON, lf	5	2	2
Mays, cf	6	1	4	Cepeda, 1b	3	0	0
McCovey, 1b	4	1	1	Lum, lf	2	0	0
Dietz, c	5	0	2	Millan, 2b	5	0	3
Henderson, lf	2	0	0	King, c	4	0	0
Fuentes, 2b	4	0	1	Williams, 3b	4	0	0
Hamilton, p	0	0	0	Perez, ss	4	1	1
McMahon, p	0	0	0	Reed, p	2	0	0
Johnson, p	0	0	0	Garrido, ph	1	0	0
Lanier, 3b	4	1	1	Priddy, p	1	0	0
Perry, p	3	0	0	Barber, p	0	0	0
Gallagher, 3b	2	0	0		—	—	—
Totals	43	6	14	Totals	41	5	11

```
San Francisco ............ 0 0 3   0 1 0   1 0 0   1—6
Atlanta .................. 2 0 2   0 0 0   1 0 0   0—5
```

E—Perry, McCovey. RBI—Bonds, Mays 2, McCovey 2, Dietz, Garr, AARON 3, Millan. LOB—San Francisco 13, Atlanta 8. 2B—Aaron, Mays. 3B—Perez. HRS—Aaron (8), McCovey (3). SB—Henderson, Millan 2. SF—McCovey.

	IP.	H.	R.	ER.	BB.	SO.
Perry (L)	5 2/3	8	5	5	1	5
Hamilton	1	1	0	0	0	1
McMahon	1/3	0	0	0	1	0
Cumberland	1 2/3	2	0	0	0	0
Johnson	1/3	0	0	0	0	0
Reed	7	9	5	5	4	4
Priddy (W)	2 2/3	5	1	1	1	3
Barber	1/3	0	0	0	0	1

Roberto Clemente's Farewell Hit

Roberto Clemente was Puerto Rico's greatest national hero. He lost his life on December 31, 1972, in the crash of a cargo plane carrying relief supplies to victims of an earthquake in Managua, Nicaragua. Puerto Rico was plunged into a period of mourning for Clemente, who had been the leader of the island's efforts to aid the surviving Nicaraguan earthquake victims.

A four-engined DC-7 piston-powered plane carrying Clemente and four other men bound for the Central American nation crashed moments after takeoff from San Juan International Airport at 9:22 p.m. of New Year's Eve. The plane came down in heavy seas about a mile and a half from shore. Vera Clemente, Roberto's wife, expressed apprehension before her husband took off. She was concerned because the plane was old and seemed to be overloaded. But Roberto assured her everything would be all right.

In eighteen seasons with the Pittsburgh Pirates, Clemente, thirty-eight years old at the time of his death, wrote one of the greatest chapters in baseball history. He was drafted from the organization of the Brooklyn Dodgers, then one of the sport's perennial powers, by the Pirates, one of baseball's lowliest teams, in 1953 for only $4000. It was one of the great bargains on record.

Roberto won the National League batting championship four times, reaching a one-season high mark of .357 in 1967. He was a member of the All-Star team

147

a dozen times and was voted the Most Valuable Player in the National League for 1966. He also was one of the finest defensive rightfielders of all time, and his throwing arm was feared throughout the League.

Clemente was the outstanding individual performer in the 1971 World Series, which was won by Pittsburgh over Baltimore. In the seven games, Roberto batted .414 on twelve hits for twenty-nine times at bat, and made several brilliant plays in the field.

Clemente, who was born August 18, 1934, at Carolina, Puerto Rico, suffered an injury-plagued 1972 season but reached a major career milestone late in the year. On September 30, 1972, he became the eleventh player in major league history to reach the three-thousand-hit plateau.

Number three thousand was Roberto's one-hundred-eighteenth hit of 1972 and was, as it turned out, the last hit he made in baseball. The Pirates were preparing for the post-season championship playoffs when they met the New York Mets at Three Rivers Stadium in a day game before 13,117 fans.

Both teams were scoreless until the fourth inning. But Clemente launched a three-run uprising for Pittsburgh when he doubled in the bottom of the fourth off New York left-hander Jon Matlack. That was his three-thousandth base hit and he eventually scored the Pirates' first run. Pittsburgh went on to win the game, 5-0. Matlack, the pitcher off whom Roberto delivered his historic hit, was the eventual choice of baseball writers as the National League's Rookie of the Year for 1972.

Clemente was the complete player. He ended his career with a lifetime batting average of .317, highest among all players who competed in the majors in 1972. His destiny was baseball, even though his father, a foreman on a sugar plantation, originally had pointed Roberto toward engineering. At seventeen, young Clemente was so outstanding a baseball prospect that his father realized it was useless to try to prevent his son from realizing his athletic potential.

Roberto fulfilled more than an athletic potential. He nursed a dream of creating a "Sports City" within Puerto Rico that would encourage youngsters to compete in athletics. It was a project that required financing, and Clemente actively sought sources for financing and contributed much of his own money toward fulfilling his dream.

When he took off for Nicaragua on New Year's Eve, he expected to be gone only a short time. Roberto told his wife and some friends he would return in time for a celebration to usher in the New Year. The day after New Year's, he was scheduled to greet Joe Brown, general manager of the Pirates, who was flying to Puerto Rico to offer his superstar his contract for 1973.

Clemente's death created a huge gap in the Pirate outfield, but no bigger than the gap created in Puerto Rico and throughout the world of professional sports by his loss.

Saturday, September 30, 1972, at Pittsburgh

New York				Pittsburgh			
	AB.	**R.**	**H.**		**AB.**	**R.**	**H.**
Garrett, 3b	4	0	0	Goggin, 2b	4	0	2
Boswell, 2b	4	0	1	Stennett, cf	4	0	0
Milner, lf	3	0	0	CLEMENTE, rf	2	1	1
Staub, rf	3	0	0	Mazeroski, ph	1	0	0
Rauch, p	0	0	0	Davalillo, rf	1	0	0
Marshall, ph	1	0	0	Stargell, 1b	3	1	1
Kranepool, 1b	3	0	1	Zisk, lf	1	2	0
Fregosi, ss	3	0	0	Sanguillen, c	3	1	1
Schneck, cf	3	0	0	Pagan, 3b	3	0	0
Dyer, c	2	0	0	Hernandez, ss	3	0	1
Nolan, c	1	0	0	Ellis, p	2	0	0
Matlack, p	2	0	0	Clines, ph	1	0	0
Hahn, ph-rf	0	0	0	Johnson, p	0	0	0
Totals	29	0	2	Totals	28	5	6

```
New York ...................... 0 0 0   0 0 0   0 0 0—0
Pittsburgh .................... 0 0 0   3 0 2   0 0 x—5
```

	IP.	H.	R.	ER.	BB.	SO.
Matlock (L, 14-10)	6	5	5	3	5	5
Rauch	2	1	0	0	0	1
Ellis (W, 15-7)	6	1	0	0	2	5
Johnson	3	1	0	0	1	2

Error—Garrett. RBI—Hernandez 2, Sanguillen. DP—New York 3. LOB—New York 5, Pittsburgh 4. 2B—Clemente. 3B—Hernandez. Passed Ball—Dyer, Nolan. Umpires—Crawford, Harvey, Kibler and Pulli. Time—2:10. Att.—13,117.